Endorsers

Every American needs to read "Th[   ]
because it exposes the specific [   ] are being
used right now to turn America into an Islamic state. As a
former Muslim, who was a professor at Al-Azhar Islamic
University, I know from experience that what this book says
is true. As we pray, "God <u>bless</u> America," let us also pray,
"God <u>protect</u> America."

Dr. Mark A. Gabriel
Author of <u>Islam and Terrorism</u>

"The Islamization of America" is an exciting and timely book
that exposes a danger which threatens America and the
whole world. The subject of the book is Islam which, when it
first started in Mecca, it was conciliatory with Christianity.
But, after relocating to Medina, it was transformed into a
totalitarian ideology that used terror to dominate the world
and subjugate populations to the Islamic law, Sharia. This
book is to read and to meditate upon.

Father Pierre Janho
The Catholic Church, Montreal, Canada

"The Islamization of America" is certainly a timely book to
exhort and warn the American people concerning the
Muslims' strategy to Islamize America. This is a book that
should be promoted by every Christian in America. It is a
most needed book.

Dr. Labib Mikhail
Author of <u>Islam, Mohammed and the Koran</u>

It is with great pleasure that I recommend "<u>The Islamization</u>
<u>of America</u>" by Brother Abdullah. He tells the truth and his
warnings should be headed by all freedom-loving
Americans.

Dr. Robert Morey
Executive Director,
Research and Education Foundation

Islamization is more than religious proselytizing; it is an ideological movement with political and cultural implications. Militant Islam's goal is the global imposition of Shari'a and Islamic dominance. Historically, Islamization has had disastrous consequences on the indigenous cultures of the societies where it has succeeded. Principles of individual freedom and pluralism are viewed with hostility; religious minorities succumb to a state of dhimmitude (institutionalized discrimination). "The Islamization of America" introduces American readers to the ideological challenge facing western values of freedom, human rights, and religious tolerance. Abdullah al-Araby makes an important contribution to public dialogue about militant Islam and American society.

Fr. Keith Roderick
Secretary General
Coalition for the Defense of Human Rights

Long before other "experts" on Islam began to speak out, write and expose the dangers inherent in this counterfeit religion, Brother Abdullah Al-Araby was courageously presenting the "truth in love." His brain child was a series of well-written brochures tackling the subject in a clear and concise fashion. "The Islamization of America" is an excellent exploration and exposition of this timely subject and worthy of reading for anyone interested in what is happening to America in the religious and intellectual fields. We have been targeted and assaulted by Islamists not only thru terrorism but also misinformation and deception. What can one do? Read this book to find out.

Anis Shorrosh, D. Min., D. Phil.
Member of Oxford Society of Scholars, Oxford, England
Author of best-seller Islam Revealed

The Islamization of America

THE ISLAMIC STRATEGIES
AND
THE CHRISTIAN RESPONSE

Abdullah Al-Araby

THE PEN VS. THE SWORD
Los Angeles, California, USA

Quotations of the Quran are from: <u>The Noble Quran</u>; By Abdullah Youssef Ali.
http://www.usc.edu/dept/MSA/quran/

Quotations of the Hadith are from: <u>The Translation of the Sahih Al-Bukhari</u>; Muhammed Muslim Khan, Lahore, Kazi Publication, 1979.

Quotations of the Bible are from: <u>The Holy Bible in the King James Version</u>. Nashville, Thomas Nelson, 1976.

First Printing
February, 2003

THE PEN vs. THE SWORD
P.O. Box 661336
Los Angeles, CA 90066
E-mail: TheTruth@aol.com

ISBN 0-9656683-7-1

Printed in the United States of America

Table of Contents

Dedication

To my precious grandchildren

*May you, and the future generations of America,
never have to go through what I once did.*

*May you never have to flee America
because it turned to Islam.*

A Bishop Living in an Islamic Country Speaks.

The problem of Islam in Europe, today and in the future

Remarks recently made by His Exc. Most Rev. Giuseppe Germano Bernardini, O.F.M. Cap., Archbishop of Izmir, in relation to Islam's invasion of European society.

I have been living in Turkey for the past 42 years. It is a 99.9% Muslim country. I have been serving as the Archbishop of Izmir, Asia Minor, for the past 16 years. My concern about today's theme is therefore obvious. There is a need for some form of intervention with regard to the problem of Islam in Europe, today and in the future. I thank Msgr. Pelâtre, who has already spoken on this theme to this prestigious assembly. His speech dispenses me of the necessity for a long examination and relative interpretations.

Above all, I am convinced that we need to humbly request that the Holy Father assist us in this intervention. To be brief and clear, I will first mention three cases. I believe these to be factual, as the sources are completely reliable.

- During an official meeting on Islamic-Christian dialogue, an authoritative Muslim person, speaking to the Christians participating, stated very calmly and assuredly: *"Thanks to your democratic laws we will invade you; thanks to our religious laws we will dominate you."*

  This is to be believed because the *dominion* has already begun with *petro-dollars*. These funds are not used to create work in poor North African or Middle Eastern countries. Rather, they are used to build mosques and cultural centers in Christian countries that permit Islamic immigration. This includes Rome, the center of Christianity. In light of this, how can we ignore that it is a clear program of expansion and re-conquest?

- The organizers of Islamic-Christian meetings in Europe are always Christians. During one such meeting, a Christian participant publicly asked the Muslims present why they did not organize at least one meeting of this kind. The Muslim authority present answered with the following words: *"Why should we? You have nothing to teach us and we have nothing to learn."*

  What value is a dialogue among deaf persons? It is a fact that terms such as "dialogue," "justice," "reciprocity," and concepts such as "rights of man" and "democracy" have completely different meanings for Muslims than they do for us. I believe the time has come for all of us to recognize and admit this.

- There is a Catholic monastery in Jerusalem that once employed, and perhaps still does, a Muslim Arab servant. He was an honest and gentle person that was greatly respected by the Christian ministers. He, in turn, respected them. One day, he sadly told them: *"Our chiefs have met and have decided that all the 'infidels' must be killed, but do not fear because I will kill you without making you suffer."*

We are all aware that we must make a distinction between the fanatic and violent minority and the tranquil and honest majority. But, we must also understand that an order given in the name of Allah, or the Quran always has the potential to make both march unified, compactly, without hesitation. Anyway, history teaches us that determined minorities always managed to impose themselves upon the convictions of the silent majority.

We would be naive to underestimate or, worse yet, smile at the three cases to which I have referred. I feel that we must reflect upon their dramatic teachings.

Despite the appearance, this is not pessimism on my part. The Christian cannot be pessimistic because Christ is Risen and Alive. He is God, as opposed to all other prophets or those calling themselves such. The final victory will be Christ's, but God's timing is often long. Meantime, He is patient and waits for the conversion of sinners. He invites the Church to organize herself and to work to quicken the coming of His Kingdom.

I now would like to make a serious proposal to the Holy Father, to organize as soon as possible, if not a Synod, at least a Symposium of Bishops. This will be for operators in the pastoral ministry for immigrants, with particular reference to those who are Muslims. This will widen the scope of the Reformed and Orthodox Churches. Its organization could be entrusted to the CCEE., in collaboration with the KEK. It has had a great deal of experience regarding this matter.

The symposium could be useful to deepen our understanding, in a collegial way, of the problem of Islamic people in Christian countries. It thus could help find a common strategy to face and resolve the problem in a Christian and objective manner. We must agree on the principles, even if their applications vary depending on the places and the persons. Nothing is worse than disagreement on principles!

I end this exhortation with a suggestion that has come to me by experience: Do not ever allow Muslims to use a Catholic Church for their cult. In their eyes, this would be the certain proof of our apostasy.

Introduction

ISLAM INVADES AMERICA

The forces of Mohammed have arrived in America, and the battle for the heart and soul of America is already in progress.

A large army of Muslim activists are working fervently at their goal. It is nothing less than converting Americans to Islam and turning America into an Islamic State. Sadly, in this battle, the most powerful nation on earth is losing ground.

Over the past generation, America has welcomed the immigration of Muslims with benign and malignant intentions. Our historic naiveté dictated that we fling open our doors without challenging those who were knocking for entrance. Clueless to their hidden agendas, we welcomed them to launch an invasion into the very fabric of our civilization.

The new Islamic invasion of America is unlike those of the early stages of Islam when they conquered most of the world with the sword. Present-day Islamic activists are much too clever to attempt taking America militarily. They fully realize that the only way to conquer us is from within. A remark made by the Libyan dictator Moammar Gaddafi reflects this reality, "*Our confrontation with America used to be like confronting a fortress from outside. Today, we have found a loophole to enter the fortress and to confront it from within.*"

Knowing that a military assault would prove fruitless, they are attempting to capture our souls by building political influence and by beguiling our citizens to convert to Islam. In this event America's land and resources will automatically fall to them as an added bonus.

Many Americans are oblivious to the fact that the Islamic invasion of America has already begun and it is slowly but surely making significant progress. This is accomplished by a large army of activists that have an arsenal consisting of a broad diversity of weapons. Tragically, the most strategic weapons that they possess are the ones that we handed them. These weapons are our democratic laws and our tolerance for all religions.

We have been duped because a wave of Muslims warriors infiltrated the ranks of the good Muslims posing as advocates of a peaceful religion. The deception led us to presume that Islam was simply a religion. We have been slow in discovering that it is actually a way of life that demands the allegiance of a nation's entire population.

Until the terrorist events of recent years, few Americans have questioned the true nature of Islam. Since September 11, 2001, we became aware that a second wave of Muslim warriors had been able to slip through our gates. These do not possess the patience or the sophisticated sneakiness of the first invaders. These new warriors came to terrorize, maim, kill and destroy. Their aim is to bring America to her knees in an immediate and agonizing defeat.

Curiously, this second wave has not spoiled the strategy for the initial peaceful invaders. The terrorism of the second group prompts those of the first group who claim that Islam is a peaceful religion to scream **constitutional foul** when our authorities seek the right to investigate Islamic groups that might be aiding and abetting terrorists. This leaves America in an awkward position with her hands tied. It is the fulfillment of a strategy that an Islamic cleric cited to the Archbishop of Izmir, *"Thanks to your democratic laws we will invade you; thanks to our religious laws we will dominate you."*

The latter group is honest only in that they are giving us a glimpse of the true nature of militant Islam. Unfortunately, their brutal honesty will be of no avail unless Americans find a way to still the protests of the peaceful invaders who tie us to political correctness whenever we attempt to protect ourselves.

Sadly, the majority of Americans fail to see the picture. They are still under the influence of the strategy of the members of the first group that came in to give us an Americanized version of Islam. These are the Muslim activists who came to us preaching a version of Islam that had been carefully revised and polished in order to subtly persuade us to embrace Islam.

Both groups have one goal in common: They want us to surrender to the will of Allah by becoming Muslims, thusly subjugating America and her resources to Islam.

The idea for this book originated from my hope of alerting America to this goal.

However, this book is not about Muslims and it is not to be used as a tool to bash them. The majority of Muslims living in the United States are peace-loving people who are contributing to its prosperity. Many of them are ignorant of the full implications of what the Quran says and what Mohammed actually taught.

This book was written to expose the covert strategy of Muslim activists for the Islamization of America. It is not meant to be just another book about Islam. It reflects my heart's cry to offer America an eye-opener and a wake-up call. My prayer is that it will serve as a guide for enacting action plans that will challenge the Islamic invasion of our country and our civilization before it is too late.

I would like to express my appreciation to all who have contributed to the production of this book. I offer my heart-felt thanks for their valued suggestions and feedback. I owe a special debt of gratitude to my good friend Rev. Jim Croft, Pastor of Gold Coast Christian Church of Boca Raton, for the extensive and intriguing foreword he wrote for the book, for his valuable insights and tireless efforts in editing this text.

Abdullah Al-Araby

Foreword

Baptized & Islamized

Islam's Subtle Assault on America's Christian Culture

By Jim Croft

It is my joy and privilege to write this foreword to my good friend's newest book, *The Islamization of America*. Over the years, Abdullah Al-Araby has become many Christian American's valued authority on Islamic issues. I know that you will find the book that you have in hand a treasury of insights into the Islamic mind. This book will serve as your eye-opener to the viable threat that Islam expansionism is to our Christian heritage.

If this generation's American Christians do not wake up, our grandchildren could easily be giving testimonies in mosques rather than churches. "Like my parents, I was baptized as a traditional Christian. But now, *Alhamdo Lillah* (thanks be to Allah), I have accepted Allah as the only God and Mohammed as Allah's Apostle and I'm now one of the millions of Americans that have been Islamized." Unthinkable? Yes! Impossible? Not unless history has stopped repeating itself.

The nations pictured in our Bible maps that were the cradle of the Christian faith have few biblically-oriented Gospel-proclaiming churches left. Instead, they have mosques. These countries include Israel, Jordan, Syria and Turkey. The nations of North Africa, stretching from Egypt westward through Libya and Algeria and on to Morocco, were once bastions of Christianity. They all fell under Islam by the 10th century. The present-day descendants of the early Christians, unlike their forefathers, are languishing as Muslims in the grip of the anti-Christ spirit of Islam. The seven cities addressed by the Spirit of Christ in the book of Revelation that were once flourishing with saved, baptized Christians, have been Islamized.

All of the aforementioned punctuate a reality to which most Americans are oblivious. Tragically, the reality is that history does repeat itself even within the Church. Islamization occurred in most of the countries that were evangelized by the Apostles within 750 years after they were initially churched. It is naïve for us to presumptuously boast that it cannot happen in the United States 1250 years later.

Eye Salve Needed to Cure Spiritual Blindness

Some might protest, "But you don't understand about the Church in America, we are in the midst of revival. Sinners are being saved, believers are being filled with the Holy Spirit, and signs and wonders are being performed in the church." All of these precious signs were far more prevalent and powerful in the early centuries of

Christianity. They did not immunize future generations from Islamization. Apparently somewhere along the line, the descendants of the early Christians spiraled into a state of prideful complacency. Like the Laodicean church, they were deceived into believing that they "had their act together" in regards to the Christian life (Rev. 3:14-19). They had become spiritually blind and needed a dose of the eye salve that Jesus had offered their ancestors. The Muslims conquered the Bible Land through their Jihad for world domination. Most citizens who refused to convert perished by the sword. Subsequently, the hostage Christian cultures of the ancient Middle East and Asia Minor began to identify with the customs of their captors and became Islamized. Increasing numbers, from generation to generation, caved in under the pressures of discrimination. Finally, all but a remnant, gullibly accepted the Muslim claims that Islam was a fulfilling extension of Christianity. Spiritual blindness prevented Christians from understanding what Islamization would mean for the future of their cultures. It cost them their faith and their values. Islam was powerless to equip them with the ability to create the innovative technologies that would be necessary to keep up pace with the western world in future generations. America will have a similar fate unless we stop the invasion of Islam in America.

Moderate's Moderation Maybe Mythological

Inevitably, whenever Islam is mentioned in a negative context, many quickly challenge that only a small minority is dangerous radicals and that the majority is harmless moderates. I believe that the facts disprove this oversimplified distinction. Islam works as a two-edged sword. One edge is terrorism and the other is the subtle process that leads to Islamization. The latter edge is comprised of moderates that, wittingly and unwittingly, work hand-in-hand with the terrorists in America.

This is how it works. The extremists commit acts of terrorism against us. The moment that our authorities begin to investigate Islamic communities for hidden terror cells and supporters, the moderates charge us with religious and race discrimination. Thus, they use our democratic laws against us. This thwarts our investigative efforts to defend ourselves and opens the door for more terrorists to invade our shores. The success of moderates in manipulating our system enables them to be perceived as a valuable voting block by prospective candidates for public office. This multiplies their potential to have ever-increasing influence over our government. Few Americans understand that Islam inherently demands what is called a "sacral government." The vernacular for this is a "Church-State" form of rule. A moderate Muslim does not qualify as a sincere Muslim unless he concurs with the Quran and every Islamic law. Fundamentalist Muslims do not consider a Muslim who voices complaints against other Muslims as a true believer. This is why there has been an absence of public Muslim protests about the Islamic terrorist crimes that have been perpetrated within our nation.

Moderate Muslims in Islamic nations cooperate with the radicals by default. Even when the moderates are in the majority, the extremists are far more proactive and politically powerful. Their radical clergymen emphasize the intolerant laws as much as they do the more rational ones. This incites their followers to organize public demonstrations that demand that the whole society legalistically adhere to all of the laws as a means of invoking the blessings of Allah on the nation. They authoritatively proclaim that they know all there is to know about what Mohammed said and what the will of Allah is for everyone else. All of this intimidates the moderates who just want to live and let live. They melt under the intensity and give lip service to whatever the extremists are prescribing.

Our politically correct news media and Muslim activist spokesmen have conditioned us with perceptions that may contain significant elements of inaccuracy. They assert that the majority of the citizens living in Islamic states are harmless moderates that have no sympathy for the terrorists. This is belied by reports that post 9/11 the first name of Bin Laden, "Osama," has attained a favored name status for newborn male infants in a dozen or more Muslim countries. In some nations, 7 out of 10 baby boys are the namesakes of the terrorist. Unless only radicals are bearing children, there are two other possibilities. Many moderates are curiously enamored with and supportive of Bin Laden's exploits. The degree of moderation of the moderates living in Islamic countries has been exaggerated.

It is my conviction that in reality there are three types of Muslims. They are the radicals, the moderates, and the westernized. The majority of those inhabiting America are likely the westernized variety. These love our nation and have wholeheartedly embraced our Judeo-Christian values. They understand the opportunities that are afforded them here could never be realized in a Muslim-ruled country. For these, the pursuit of happiness is primary, their religion a meaningless coincidence of birth. In my estimation there is only one variety of Muslims who are guaranteed would never wittingly aid and abet terrorists or cooperate with schemes to Islamize us. It is the westernized. Rarely could any member of this group be unwittingly lured into schemes of duplicity, as they have learned to regard fellow Muslims with suspicion.

Doctrines of Demons and the Spirit of Anti-Christ

Who was the Allah of Islam? Mohammed adopted the name from the polytheistic Arabs who were his contemporaries. Allah was the chief of their 360 gods. The attributes of Allah are incompatible with those of the Loving Father God of the Bible. The Apostle Paul warned Christians that Satan could transform into an angel of light. He also said that he was concerned about those who would come preaching under the inspiration of a spirit that was different from the Holy Spirit. These would declare a different Gospel that would feature another Christ ("anointed one of God"). His concern was that many would be deceived into departing from authentic faith in Christ by listening to the doctrines of demons that were based on lies (2 Cor. 11:1-4, 14 & 1 Tim. 4:1-2).

All of this describes the events that spawned Islam. An angel of light ("light" is a synonym for "revelation") came to Mohammed and said that he was both Gabriel and the Holy Spirit. This mixture definitely makes this being of an entirely different spiritual species than the divine, eternal Holy Spirit of God. Mohammed was deceived into believing that he was superior in anointing to Christ. This would infer a different Christ, or anointed one. The prophet then began to proclaim the demonic doctrinal lie that he had a religion that was "better news" for mankind than the Gospel of Jesus (The word *gospel* means *good news*.) So he was surely preaching a different Gospel. Therefore, the spiritual entity that gave revelations to Mohammed was at best a lying, deceiving spirit and at worst Satan, the father of lies, acting as an angel of light.

Anyone that is familiar with the Bible and reads either the Quran or the Hadith can discern that Mohammed was familiar with Judaism and Christianity and that he borrowed generously from their writings. Mohammed made the self-aggrandizing claim that he was Allah's final messenger with divine insights and an anointing that eclipsed those of his predecessors. According to the Christian Bible, Mohammed can be identified as a deceived deceiver that was operating under the influence of a spirit of antichrist. The prefix *anti* of the word *antichrist* can mean *in place of* as well as *against*. The word *Christ* is defined as *the anointed one of God*. Therefore, a reasonable expanded definition of the word *antichrist* might read, *one who is operating in an anointing that is a substitute for the true anointing* (Heb. 1:1-3 & 1 John 4:1-3). Mohammed espoused teachings that denied the divine Sonship of Jesus. In 1 John 2:22, it says that anyone that denies the Father and the Son is a liar and antichrist. The Muslim mosque in Jerusalem is called the Mosque of Omar. It bears an Arabic inscription that defies the Father and Son relationship between God and Jesus. It says, "Allah has no son."

The Clash of Cultures

Americans suffer from prideful naivety. We actually believe that the whole world is obligated to think as we do about the basic issues of life. The following contrasts will show that the Islamic mind is in diametric opposition to the Judeo-Christian values that we hold dear. Should we give in to Islamization, future generations of our citizens will also routinely accept things that we currently abhor.

One's Word Being One's Bond vs. the Prevalence of Duplicity

Americans frequently seal contracts with a handshake. An individual who regularly tells even little white lies is regarded as having a questionable character. The fabric of our family, educational, and business institutions would be severely compromised if we abandoned this value. There is an Islamic principle called *Al Takeyya*. It does not merely make a provision for telling lies; it actually encourages it. Muslims are permitted to utilize this principle whenever confronted with the following situations: to spread the influence of Islam; to protect one's own welfare; to reconcile quarrelers; and to appease one's spouse.

Redemptive Criminal Punishment vs. Human Rights Infractions

We are the kindest of nations to criminals. Our goal is inevitably rehabilitation. Islamic penal practices deal with such people differently. Thieves are sentenced to hand amputation. People charged with adultery and fornication are flogged and, in some instances, stoned. I once prayed for a man about shameful sexual sins that he had committed while living in Turkey. He had frequented Turkish prisons where women prisoners earned their keep by prostitution. I personally witnessed a young boy being beaten to death in Nigeria for the crime of shoplifting. The offenses of speaking against Islamic authorities, the Quran, or Mohammed are considered blasphemous and are punishable by execution. I recently read an account of 12 young men that were charged with being traitors to Islam in Dacca, Bangladesh. 20,000 men and women cheered as soldiers led them into the center of a stadium's field. The soldiers bayoneted each of them in the chest and abdomen. The crowd chanted, "Allah Akbar," and filed down in an orderly manner to where the men lay in their death pangs. One by one, the crowd took turns stomping on the men. The men's bodies were disintegrated into pulverized masses of flesh, blood, and bones. Only a demonized religion could incite humans to act in such a barbarous manner.

Equal Rights vs. Gender Bias

Women have long worked to earn their right to equality in the United States. They have achieved voting rights, the privilege of higher education, and are slowly being rewarded equal vocational pay. Married women cannot be forced to have sexual relations with their husbands. Divorced women are awarded alimony in most states and are guaranteed half of their husbands' assets. They routinely get the custody of children when marriages are dissolved. Widowed women in America control a gigantic portion of its financial resources. Not so under Islam. Voting and equal educational rights are rarely afforded to women. A wife is considered to be her husband's possession. In matters of divorce, a mother is apt to lose custody of her children and the potential for financial support. Widows are not the first consideration when it comes to inheriting their husband's estates.

The Honor of the Marriage Bed vs. Abominable Sexual Practices

In our present culture marital fidelity to one spouse at a time is honored. Infidelity, premarital sex, and homosexuality may be frowned upon, but are not offenses that bear dire consequences. Prostitution is in most cases a punishable crime. Rape and heterosexual/homosexual pedophilia are absolutely forbidden and bear the consequence of imprisonment. Under Islam, adulterers are stoned and unmarried fornicators are flogged. Even though polygamy is allowed for men, encounters with prostitutes are legitimized for them by a concept called *Zawag al-Mutaa* in Arabic. Literally translated, it means "marriage for pleasure." It is a temporary marriage that can last for as little as an hour, or a day, or a month, or whatever. The men pay the women mutually agreed sums of money for the pleasure that they anticipate. When Pakistan defeated Bangladesh in 1971, Pakistani soldiers raped 250,000 girls and women. They could do so without shame due to the cultural absolutions available to them through Islam. Soldiers of Christianized nations would have been executed for this offense.

One of the most horrifying aspects of Islam is that it rationalizes what we would term as nothing less than pedophilic rape. A high value is placed on wives coming to the marriage bed as virgins. To insure chastity, girls are often given in marriage between the ages of 9 and 11. The moment the girls reach puberty their husbands engage in sexual intercourse with them. The men are often 30 years senior to their little wives. For these hapless children their first sexual experiences amount to frightening rapes. Homosexual pedophilia is also acceptable in some Islamic countries. The following is an abbreviation of a journalist's observations. He was invited to attend a wedding in the United Arab Emirates where, to his surprise, a sheikh was marrying an eleven-year-old boy. Someone felt that an explanation was in order. The guests were told that it was important that a prominent sheikh have a few boys in his harem. To validate that this was acceptable, he recited two verses from the Quran, *"And there shall wait on them young boys of their own, as fair as virgin pearl."* (52:24) *"They shall be attended by boys graced with eternal youth who to the beholders eyes will seem like sprinkle pearls."* (76:19)

The journalist continued his report by stating that an Egyptian court had recently prosecuted thirty young homosexuals, as homosexuality is prohibited in Islam. A summarization of his thoughts could go along this line: "One wonders, if homosexuality is prohibited, then why Allah promises that men that were good Muslims while alive, will have young boys as sex partners in Paradise? It must be that in instances like the Emirate Sheikh's intended pedophilic sex with his male child bride, it is not considered to be homosexuality. It is permissible in that it is merely pedophilia. If two mutually consenting men have sex, it is the sinful crime of homosexuality."

Interfaith Tolerance vs. Contemptuous Intolerance

Most of our Christian clergymen are ecumenically sensitive. They enjoy participating in interfaith dialogues in their quest to bring more understanding between the various religions represented in their communities. After 9/11, many rushed to reassure local imams (Muslim clergy) that there would be no retaliation against their followers and mosques. Some denominational groups have been known to offer their church facilities to Muslims that have mosques under construction. In thirty years of public ministry, I have not encountered a single report of Muslims reciprocating to Christian generosity by offering their facilities to fellowships that needed a meeting hall.

The extent of Islam's contemptuous intolerance for Christianity and Judaism is legendary. These groups are not allowed to refurbish houses of worship or build new ones in most Muslim countries without first obtaining a presidential decree. It is a well-known fact that after the Israelis reclaimed Jerusalem in the Six-Day War, they were faced with an exhaustive clean-up project at the site of Herod's temple. For years the local Muslim Arabs have been using the base of the Wailing Wall as a public toilet. This was nothing less than an intentional assault on the Jew's spiritual history.

The Italian journalist, Oriana Fallaci, authored a book entitled *Rage and Pride*. It vented her rage relating to the pervasive manner in which Europeans are succumbing to Muslim efforts to Islamize the Christian culture of Europe. In vivid, vernacular terms she described how offended she was about immigrant Somali Muslims defiling the grounds of a cathedral in Florence, Italy. They stained the marble edifice with their urine and filled the exterior entrance to the Bishop's Baptistery with their excrement. She stated that she was equally outraged about the chimes of church bells being obliterated by taped cries of muezzins calling the faithful to prayer five times daily.

Peaceful Assembly vs. Violent Protest

United States citizens rarely demonstrate their displeasure over religious issues by rioting. Antagonists can shout that God is dead. Wayward theologians can write that Jesus was born a Roman soldier's bastard and that he fornicated with Mary Magdalene in adulthood. These will draw little more than a few fiery Sunday sermons to the guiltless sitting in churches during the following weeks. At worst, there might be a spattering of peaceful protesters carrying placards at a few sites around the country. There is something virulent about the nature of Islam that incites its adherents to violence. This phenomenon is not restricted to Arab Muslims. If authority figures of Christian democracies utter even a hint of disrespect for Mohammed or the Quran, Mullahs start issuing death decrees. Violent riots ensue in every nation that has a significant Muslim population - Indonesia, Pakistan, India, Africa, and the Middle East alike. If Islam gains much more ground in the United States, our abilities to exercise freedom of speech and the press will be significantly altered.

The First Amendment's Division of Church and State vs. a State Religion

Our founding fathers authored the First Amendment to the Bill of Rights. The intention was to protect us against the event that some sect within Christianity might attempt to wield heavy influence in the affairs of state. The citizens of the thirteen colonies sighed with relief. Most of them were the descendants of those that had fled Europe because of persecutions by Church-State governments. In addition, many clergymen were coming to the understanding that New Testament-based theology provides overwhelming indications that the affairs of the Church and the State are to be kept separate. All willing accepted the amended legislation as it was written. The problem is neither our founding fathers nor their constituents had a clue about the expansionist mentality of Islam. Their perceptions could not calculate that hordes of Muslims would be immigrating to our shores. There was no anticipation of the invasion of an anti-Christian religion that would have an inherent theological predisposition to establish a Religious State government. Even more so, they did not imagine that any religious group could use our democratic laws against us. As brilliant as they were, nobody expected that acts of terror by one segment of a religion could be collaborated with the efforts of that religion's peaceful segment to gain an advantage over us. Nobody foresaw that a culture marinated in Christian values was at risk of being Islamized within 300 years.

Americans must become aware of the alarming progress that Muslims are making in Islamizing the Christian cultures of the world around us. In the United Kingdom, they are a strong enough block to demand that the government finance the building of mosques. In the United States and Canada they are petitioning school boards to grant Muslim children the right to kneel and recite Islamic prayers in hallways while schools are in session. Hundreds of millions of petrodollars are flowing into our nation to finance mosques and Islamic educational departments in our state universities.

All of the aforementioned are part of a clever scheme. The abundance of mosques, muezzins heard calling people to prayer and thousands kneeling publicly in prayer five times daily will have a desensitizing effect. We will begin to lose sight of the reality that such are not part and parcel of our traditional Judeo-Christian culture. This paves the way for the Islamization of America.

The efforts of Muslims to obliterate the future of our Christian heritage maybe a reality, but at this juncture, it is by no means an accomplished fact. If you prayerfully read this book it can serve as your eye salve from the Lord to open your eyes to what is happening. Then you will be well equipped to thwart Islamization from progressing further. Once you have digested the contents, do not let this book lay dormant. Pass it around to your friends, clergymen, and congressional representatives.

Jim Croft
Pastor, Gold Coast Christian Church,
Boca Raton, Florida

Chapter One

One Nation under Allah

After the collapse of communism, almost everyone heaved a sigh of relief. Many thought that all threats to our freedom had finally vanished. Unfortunately, this proved to be wishful thinking.

Today, there is a more dangerous movement that is working inside America. Its name is Islam and its goal is to convert all Americans into Muslims and transform the United States into an Islamic nation. The following statements made by Muslim leaders reflect that reality[1]:

- **Omar Abdel Rahman**, the blind sheikh, was convicted of engaging in a seditious conspiracy that included the 1993 World Trade Center attack and the foiled plot to bomb New York City landmarks, including the United Nations and the Lincoln and Holland tunnels. In 1991, the sheikh called on Muslims to *"conquer the lands of the infidels."*

- **Isma'il Al-Faruqi**, a very influential Muslim leader claimed in 1983 that *"Nothing could be greater than this youthful, vigorous, and rich continent (North America) turning away from its past evil and marching forward under the banner of Allahu Akbar (Allah is great)."*

- **Imam Siraj Wahhaj** was the first imam (Muslim clergy) to offer a Muslim prayer in the U.S. House of Representatives. Imam Siraj Wahhaj was the Imam of Masjid Al-Taqwa in Brookyn, New York. He received Imam training at Ummul Qura University of Makkah in 1978 and has gone on to become a national and international speaker on Islam. He believes that if Muslims unite, they could elect their own leader as president, *"Take my word; if 6-8 million Muslims unite in America, the country will come to us."*

- **Imam Zaid Shakir** was the former Muslim chaplain at Yale University. He is a political science professor, and very active on the Islamic speaker circuit. He believes that the Quran "pushes us in the exact opposite direction to the forces at work in the American political spectrum.*" As a result he maintains that Muslims cannot accept the legitimacy of the existing system.*

- **Ahmad Nawfal**, a well-known Jordanian speaker, says that if fundamentalist Muslims stand up, *"it will be very easy for us to preside over this world once again."*

- At a Muslim convention held in San Jose, just one month after the atrocities of Sept. 11, 2001, one of the delegates declared: *"By the year 2020, we should have an American Muslim president of the United States."*

A RELIGION AND A STATE

Islam claims more than a billion followers worldwide and is rapidly growing. This movement dictates whom one should worship, how to dress, what to eat, how to answer the call of nature, how one should invest money, how to have sex, when to beat one's wife, when one must kill, and the cause for which one should die.

Islam invaded our shores protected by our freedom of religion and has spread in every direction. It took advantage of the majority's lack of knowledge about the Arabic language and Islamic history. Islam encompasses far more than a religion; it is a comprehensive way of life. The Quran and the Hadith, Islam's holy books, contain the religious, social, civil, commercial, military, and legal codes for Muslims to follow.

The teachings of Islam are not simply ethical guidelines. They are binding laws with severe punishments attached. These punishments range from public floggings to chopping off of body parts and on through to executions by beheading.

A RELIGION OF THE SWORD

The most alarming fact about Islam is that if it is allowed to become powerful enough, people will lose their choice to either accept it or reject it. The only option is to accept it. Beyond that one can at best become a second-class citizen or, at worst, face death. Allah's instructions are clear:

> *"**Fight and slay** the Pagans wherever ye find them, and seize them, beleaguer them, and lie in wait for them in every stratagem (of war)."*   Surah 9:5

According to the Quran, there can be no toleration for another religion other than Islam in an Islamic state:

> *"If anyone desires a religion other than Islam (submission to Allah), **never will it be accepted** of him; and in the Hereafter he will be in the ranks of those who have lost."*   Surah 3:85

Some suggest that Islam speaks well about "People of the Book" (Christians and Jews).   Well, not well enough. Read on:

> *"Fight those who believe not in Allah nor the last day.. Nor acknowledge the religion of truth**, (even if they are) of the people of the Book**, until they pay the Jizya (taxes) with willing submission, and feel themselves subdued."*   Surah 9:29

A HISTORY OF TERRORISM

Muslims have been using the power of terror throughout history as they followed the instructions of Allah about how to deal with infidels. Here are just a few examples:

- o In the United States on September 11, 2001, Muslims hijackers used airplanes to destroy the Twin Towers of New York's World Trade Center and the Pentagon building in Washington D.C. More than three thousand people were killed. In 1993, Muslims bombed the World Trade Center and conspired to blow up key federal buildings and commuter tunnels.

Prior to these events they held American hostages in Iran and Lebanon.

o In Southern Sudan, Muslims have destroyed whole villages. They have killed around 2 million Christians and Animists. Leaders have been crucified in front of their people. Boys and girls have been kidnapped and sold into slavery.

o After embracing Islam, Idi Amin of Uganda slaughtered 300,000 Ugandans, most of whom were Christians.

o In Nigeria, Christians are beaten, imprisoned and killed. Converting to Islam is seen as an easy way out.

o In the lands where Christianity was born, Jordan, the West Bank, Syria and Turkey, Christianity is vanishing. If this trend continues, Christianity will completely disappear from the area within a few years.

o In 1974, the army of Muslim Turkey invaded the northern part of Cyprus, pushing some 200,000 Christian Cypriots toward the south.

o At the beginning of the 20th century, Muslim Turks massacred more than 1.5 million Armenian Christians for no apparent reason other than being Christians.

A 7TH CENTURY WAY OF LIFE

No matter how much Muslims attempt to dress up Islam to make it attractive to the West, there are still many teachings of Islam that fall short of recognized modern standards for human rights. The rights that were accorded to 7th century Bedouins are far from being acceptable to us in this 21st century.

Here are few examples of the teachings of Islam:

Men are superior to women.
*"..And women shall have rights similar to the rights against them, according to what is equitable; but **men have a degree** over them."*   Surah 2:228

Women have half the rights of men.
A- In inheritance: A woman's share is half that of a man.
*"To the male a portion equal to that of **two** females..."*
                                                                 Surah 4:11

B- In court witness: A woman's witness is worth half that of a man.
*"And get two witnesses out of your own men, and if there are not two men, then a man and **two** women such as ye choose, for witness..."*   Surah 2:282

Islam considers a wife the possession of her husband.
*"Fair in the eyes of men is the love of **things they covet**: Women and sons; heaped-up hoards of gold and silver; horses..."*   Surah 3:14

Islam teaches that it is acceptable for a husband to punish a wife by beating her and abstaining from sexual relations with her.

*"...As to those women on whose part ye fear disloyalty and ill-conduct, **admonish them, refuse to share their beds, beat them**."*   Surah 4:34

*"For those who take an oath for **abstention** from their wives, a waiting for four months is ordained; if they return, God is oft-forgiving, most merciful."*   Surah 2:226

Islam instructs women to always veil themselves when they are outside of their homes. In certain situations it is mandatory even when in their own homes.

*"And say to the believing women that they should lower their gaze and guard their modesty; that they **should not display their beauty** and ornaments except what appear thereof; that they should draw their veils over their bosoms and not display their beauty..."*   Surah 24:31

"O prophet! Tell thy wives and daughters, and the believing women, that they should cast their outer garments over their persons (when abroad)." Surah 33:59

Islam allows polygamy: A man may be married to four wives at one time.
*"...Marry women of your choice, two, or three, or **four**..."*
                    Surah 4:3

Note: Extra privileges were given to Mohammed, the prophet of Islam. He was allowed unlimited wives. We know for a fact that he had at least 13 wives in addition to several concubines.

Mohammed was fifty-three years old when he married a nine-year-old child named Ayesha. He took another wife named Zaynab Bint Jahsh who was his daughter-in-law. When her husband Zaid, Mohammed's adopted son, saw that Mohammed desired his wife, he divorced her so that Mohammed could marry her.

Islam considers the wife a sex object.
*"Your wives are as **a tilth** (a field to be ploughed) unto you, so **approach your tilth when or how ye will**."*
Surah 2:223

A man may divorce his wife by oral pronouncement. However, the Quran does not offer the same right to the wife.
*"It may be, if he **divorced** you that Allah will give him in exchange consorts better than you..."* Surah 66:5

Muslims must fight until all of their opponents submit to Islam, unless, of course, those opponents prefer to die. Christians and Jews (People of the Book [the Bible]) may be spared if they pay "Jizya" (penalty tax) with willing submission, and humiliation.
*"**Fight** those who believe not in Allah, nor the last day... Nor acknowledge the religion of truth, (even if they are) of the people of the Book, **until they pay the Jizya** (taxes) with willing submission, and feel themselves subdued."*
Surah 9:29

*"But when the forbidden months are past, then **fight and slay the pagans** wherever ye find them and seize them, beleaguer them, and lie in wait (ambush) for them in every stratagem (of war); but if they repent and establish regular prayers and practice regular charity then open the way for them."* Surah 9:5 (see also Surah 2:193)

Islam instructs Muslims not to befriend Jews or Christians.
*"O ye who believe! **Take not the Jews and the Christians for your friends** and protectors. They are but friends and protectors to each other. And he amongst you*

that turns to them (for friendship) is one of them. Allah guideth not a people unjust." Surah 5:51

Any person who accepts Islam and then later turns away from it will be subject to death.
*"But if they violate their oath after their covenant, and taunt you for your faith, **fight** ye (kill) the chiefs of unbelief: for their oaths are nothing to them."* Surah 9:12

Islam teaches that the Quran is the Constitution. God is the author of law and the State is the agent to implement God's laws. In Islam, there is no separation between Church and State.
*"**The command (the rule) is for none but Allah**; He hath commanded that ye worship none but Him: That is the right religion, but most men understand not."* Surah 12:40

Adultery and Fornication: Unmarried fornicators are punished by public floggings. Adulterers are punished by being stoned.
*"The woman and the man guilty of adultery or fornication, **flog** each of them with a hundred stripes; let not compassion move you in their case, in a matter prescribed by Allah, if ye believe in Allah and the Last Day; and let a party of the believers witness their punishment."* Surah 24:2

Stealing: Punished by amputating the hands.
*"As to the thief, male or female, **cut off his or her hands**: A punishment, by way of example, from Allah for their crime: and Allah is exalted in power."* Surah 5:38

Drinking alcohol: According to the Hadith (Mohammed's sayings) is punishable by 40 to 80 lashes.
See Sahih al-Bukhari vol. 8:770

If Islam Ruled America

Islam is more than a religion; it is a comprehensive way of life. The Holy books of Islam are the Quran (believed by Muslims to be God's word), and the Hadith (Mohammed's sayings). These books prescribe a vast number of regulations that govern every aspect of life of Muslims. Islam functions under what Christians would refer to as a sacral or Church/State form of government. For Muslims the concept that **"Islam is a religion and a State"** is an integral part of their religion.

Let us examine what Islam would do if it ruled America. What would happen to the values and institutions that our country was founded upon and we hold dear?

First: Liberty

The United States was built on its Constitution and the first ten of its Amendments known as the Bill of Rights. These were established by our Founding Fathers, who came to America to escape religious oppression. The Amendments to the Constitution give citizens the right to express themselves in any manner they please. They can criticize the President if they believe he is wrong. They can observe any form of worship that they choose. They have the freedom to act in any way they see appropriate, as long as it does not violate the rights of others.

What would happen to these freedoms in an Islamic state? Would the citizens be granted the right to choose the religion they want, or would they be forced into Islam according to this Quranic verse:
*"If any one desires a religion other than Islam, **never will it be accepted** of him, and in the hereafter he will be in the ranks of those who have lost."*   Surah 3:85

How about the right of a Muslim to change his own religion? Would he be given this right or would he be punished according to the apostasy rule which states that such a person should be punished by death? Mohammed said "*Whoever changes his religion, **kill** him.*"

Al Bukhari Vol. 9:57

Do Muslim activists want to limit us to the same rights that are granted to the citizens of Islamic countries such as Saudi Arabia? There, women are not allowed to drive automobiles and no one can observe public worship according to any religion other than Islam.

Do they want us to be ruled by a ruler such as Khomeini? He issued an order to murder the writer, Salman Rushdie, whose only crime was that he dared to criticize Islam.

Even in some moderate Islamic states, Christians have to obtain a presidential decree to build a church. They face discrimination in many aspects of life including education, employment and vocational promotions. Religious affiliation is posted to citizens' ID cards to identify the Christians and discriminate against them.

If Islam ruled America, everybody would suffer. Those who will embrace Islam would loose the freedom they once enjoyed as part of the American way of life. Should they decide to change their Islamic religion and go back to their Christian or Jewish faiths, they would be subject to death. The Christians and Jews, who will decide to keep their faith, would be treated as second-class citizens. Their freedom of worship would be restricted. Their freedom of expression would be terminated. Their right to have access to the best education and the chance to reach the top of the job ladder and hold key positions would be denied. **America would cease to be "*the land of the free.*"**

Second: Democracy

Our present system in the United States gives citizens the right to rule themselves. They can write the laws that will govern their lives, decide the amount of taxes to be collected from them and how it will be spent.

One important principle in this great system is the separation of church and state. Islam, however, is built on an opposing concept, **"Islam is a Religion and a State."** According to Islam, the Quran is the principal source of legislation:
"*We have sent down to thee the book (the Quran) in truth, that you might **judge men as guided by Allah**.*"

Surah 4:105

If the Quran is the law, what are some of the rules and regulations that will be imposed? Here are just a few examples:

- **Stealing**: Punished by hand amputation. (Surah 5:38)

- **Adultery**: Punished by public flogging (Surah 24:2) for the single man or woman. For married people, the punishment is stoning.

- **Drinking Alcohol**: Punished by 40 or 80 lashes. (Al Bukhari 8:770)

- **Resisting Islam**: Punished by death, crucifixion or the cutting off of the hands and feet. (Surah 5:33)

- Prisons in most Muslim countries are known to be centers of torture rather than rehabilitation.

Third: Equality

Under our system in the United States, there should be no discrimination among citizens based on sex, color, religion or race.

Would Islam treat men and women equally?

- When it teaches that men are superior to women. (Surah 2:228)

- When it gives men double the share that women receive in inheritances. (Surah 4:11)

- When it gives a man double the value of a woman's witness in court. Even if a woman is raped, she must have two male witnesses to collaborate her testimony. (Surah 2:282)

Would Islam treat non-Muslims fairly?

- When the Quran calls on Muslims not to befriend Jews or Christians. (Surah 5:51)

- When the Quran imposes "Jizya" (tax) on Christians and Jews that will be collected only from them and not from Muslims. (Surah 9:29)

Could Islam someday rule America?

Islam is growing rapidly in America. It is a matter of time before Islam will become the religion of the majority. America will then be labeled an "Islamic country." It will be ruled by the "Quran" and the "Hadith," or what Muslims call the "Sharia." (The Islamic code of ethics)

However, it is not necessary for Muslims to become a large majority before they can force their will on the helpless minority. While still a minority, they can become large enough to change our laws in their favor. This can be accomplished if they unite and become a strong voting block. In a true democracy, such as ours, even a minority voting block could be the deciding factor on who would become our president, legislators, governors, mayors, and so forth. They could demand concessions favoring them, and get them.

Have you, dear reader, become alarmed enough? I hope that you would. Those among us who have lived once under Islam know how bad it can get. Some of us had to flee our mother countries and take refuge in America. We dread the thought that America could fall under Islamic rule. If this occurred our children and grandchildren would have to flee America as we did in our original homelands.

The difference, this time, is that there might not be any democracies left in the world to take refuge.

Chapter Two

ON THE ROAD TO THE NEW WORLD

Muslims often claim that Islam is the world's fastest growing religion. This boast endows them with increased fervor as they race down the road toward the conquest of the New World. They argue that the number of new adherents embracing Islam is an indication of Allah's vindication and Islam's appeal as the only true religion. They ask, "How could so many people be wrong?" Hand in hand with this, Muslims cite another equally important claim, that Islam has a lower attrition rate than other faiths.

Undisputedly, Islam is growing rather rapidly, but there is no scientific evidence for the claim that Islam is the world's fastest growing religion. The purpose is not to dispute the fact that Islam is growing, but to demonstrate that the reasons for Islam's growth can be attributed to factors that have little to do with Islam's merits. To accomplish this, we will explore the reasons and implications behind the phenomenon of the spread of Islam during historical and contemporary times.

First, we will acquaint you with some of the Islamic principles that serve as the force behind Islam's expansionist mentality.

Islam's ultimate goal is to rule the world. Islamic theology provides two methods to accomplish this. **The first is spiritual**, as people are lured into conversion. **The second is coercive;** it is the political/physical conquest of nations. For Muslims, there are no gray areas. They see the world in black and white. To them the world is divided into two big camps: *the House of Islam* and *the House of War*. The House of Islam is the Muslims, and the House of war is the non-Muslims. Muslims (the House of Islam) are in a constant state of spiritual/political/physical warfare with Non-Muslims (the House of War) until they subjugate them into Islam.

Islam always employs a *carrot and stick* policy. The carrot and stick perpetually set before Muslims is the expectation of generous rewards in this life and in eternity for those who fight for Islam. On the other hand, those who falter are warned of severe temporal and eternal punishments.

Apostasy from Islam is not an option. Once-a-Muslim-always-a-Muslim, the only official alternative is death. There is no room for changing one's mind. The door is wide open to join Islam, but there is no backdoor for those that would like to leave it.

The Early Stages of Islam
Mohammed started espousing his new Islamic religion at age 40. Initially, his methods for spreading the message were gentle and peaceful. The motto was, "No compulsion in religion." His first convert was his loyal wife, Khadija. During the next three years, Mohammed privately persuaded seven men to join him, one of whom

44

was his slave Zaid. The other six were: Abu Bakr, Uthman ibn Affan, Zubair ibnel Awam, Abdel Rahman ibn Auf, Saad ibn abi Wakkaas, and Talha. With this limited success, Mohamed decided to begin preaching the message of Islam in public. During this period he was under the protection of an influential uncle named, Abu-Talib. There is no evidence, however, that his uncle ever converted to Islam. After five years of hard work, the Muslim band had grown in numbers to a total of a mere sixteen. Some of Mohammed's followers migrated to a Christianized area that is present day Ethiopia. These enthusiasts succeeded in adding only a few more men, women and children to Islam's membership. To this day, Ethiopia remains a predominantly Christian country. As the years passed, the number of Muslims in Mecca, the birthplace of Islam, grew to about forty men and women.[1]

Mohammed used every maneuver at his disposal to convince the polytheistic people of Mecca to embrace Islam. They worshipped 360 gods, of whom Allah was considered the ruling deity. To appease and appeal to the pagan Arabs, Mohammed incorporated some of their idolatrous rituals into Islam. The Islamic practices of making Hajj, circling the Kaaba, and kissing the black stone are all pagan rituals that predate Islam[2]. During one of his meetings with the chiefs of the Quraish tribe of Mecca, he took a step that exposed the depth of his deceptive desperation. He feigned devotion to their pagan deities. He recited the following Quranic verses wherein supposedly Allah praised the three pagan Arabian goddesses, *Allat*, *Al-Uzza*, and *Manat*[3]. The verses read, *"Have you not seen Allat, and Al-Uzza, and Manat, the other, the third? These are the exalted Swans, and truly their intercession may be hoped for."* Mohammed then led the Qurashites in paying homage to the goddesses by kneeling in prayer with them. Soon afterward Mohammed alleged that Satan had whispered the verses in his ears. He nullified the verses and changed the text of Surah 53:19-23 to read as it does today.

Regardless of his hard work, willingness to compromise with idolatry and peaceful preaching, nothing seemed to work in his efforts to add members to his new religion. After 13 years of being headquartered in Mecca, he had won no more than 100 converts. The failures, the ridicules and the threats against him by the people of Mecca, led him to a pivotal decision. In 622 A.D., he decided to relocate his ministry base from Mecca to Medina, Arabia. This action was so fundamental to the development of Islam that Muslims, later, marked it by a new Hijira (migration) calendar. After moving to Medina, a new revolutionary methodology for spreading the Muslim message was introduced. The days of being a peaceful, tolerant prophet were now over. **At this juncture Mohammed began to proclaim that Allah was instructing all Muslims to use swords, not just words, to fight for the cause.** They were to adopt the sword of Jihad as the primary means of subduing the masses to the will of Allah. From that point on, Mohammed's directives and the actions of his Muslim band signaled to non-Muslim Arabs that all his old peace pacts with them and former promises to them were null and void.

Soon, significant numbers of Arabs flocked to join Mohammed[4]. Their motivations for doing so were twofold. They feared his ruthlessness, and they hoped for shares of the booty derived from the Muslims' plundering of caravans and villages. Muslims conducted a series of 27 raids on other Arabian tribes and caravans in which they killed opponents and captured goods, slaves and new territories. Mohammed personally observed 26 of these raids, and participated by fighting in 9 of them. His peaceful efforts prior to the migration to Medina produced a constituency primarily comprised of friends and family. During the subsequent years, and up until his death, tens of thousands were added to the ranks of Islam through his new policy of coercive violence.

Eight years after arriving in Medina, Mohammed was able to organize an army of 10,000 to attack Mecca. For the most part, this army consisted of men that were far more motivated by personal greed for material gains than they were by spiritual zeal for Allah's call. Conversely, the Meccans who surrendered to Islam after Mohammed's victory were motivated more by fear of death than by sincere belief in Allah and his Apostle. Mohammed was successful in subduing all of Arabia under his control and at the time of his death he was planning to send an army to capture Syria. However, events that transpired over the next few years proved that the conversions of many were a matter of coercion rather than conviction. Those who perceived opportunities to forsake Islam did so with greater rapidity than their original conversions[5].

After Mohammed's death, the various factions within Arabia revolted against Islam. The successors of Mohammed were called Caliphs. The first one, Caliph Abu Bakr, had to recall the Muslim army from the anticipated conquest of Syria to quell a revolt at home. This revolt resulted in a fierce war called *the Apostasy War*, which was waged against the masses that were attempting to leave Islam. The Muslims prevailed after offering the Arabian rebels a combination of attractive enticements and physical threats[6].

Once the Arabian Peninsula was securely under Muslim control, it was time to look beyond its borders in furthering Islam's influence. Between the years 637 A.D. – 644 A.D. the second Caliph, Omar, authorized a number of successful raids to subjugate many of the neighboring countries. Egypt, Palestine, Syria, Armenia, Iraq and Iran were all invaded and Islamized.

Within a century of its birth, there were many indications that Islam was making great progress on its road to establishing a New World Order. Islamic forces raged through North Africa and destroyed corrupt Byzantine Christianity in their wake. They conquered all of the Middle East, Central Asia and large portions of India. In 710 A.D. Islamic forces crossed the Straits of Gibraltar and swept through most of Spain and Portugal. France was invaded and one-third of it was captured. Fortunately, when the Muslim hordes were 125 miles from Paris, they were defeated by Charles Martel at the Battle of Tours (Poitiers) in 732 A.D. The Muslims' occupation of Spain lasted a few hundred years until they were slowly driven back to North Africa.

Muslim activists constantly boast that "Islam is the religion of peace and tolerance." They assert that the wars of Islam were only "defensive" actions in response to the aggressions of others. Historical facts belie their assertions. The nations that the Muslims conquered did not pose any threat to Arabia. The countries that the Muslims invaded had not initiated attacks. The Muslims attacked them with the motive of prospective plunder and the desire to force Islam on the rest of the world. Allah's orders were clear, "*When the forbidden months are past, then **fight and slay the Pagans** wherever ye find them, and seize them, beleaguer them, and lie in wait for them in every stratagem (of war); but if they repent, and establish regular prayers and practice regular charity, then open the way for them: for Allah is Oft-forgiving, Most Merciful.*"   Surah 9:5

In dealing with "People of the Book" (Christians and Jews), the Quran was a bit more generous. The Quran did not call for their deaths, but commanded Muslims to, "*Fight those who believe not in Allah nor the Last Day, nor hold that forbidden which hath been forbidden by Allah and His Messenger, nor acknowledge the religion of*

Truth, (even if they are) of the People of the Book, until **they pay the Jizya with willing submission, and feel themselves subdued.**" Surah 9:29

It was no surprise that the invading Muslims were not satisfied to merely subjugate the conquered countries to Islamic Law. In addition, each nation underwent the process of Arabization. This was accomplished as the invaders systematically attempted to erase the identities of ethnic groups, by abolishing their native cultures and languages and replacing them with Arab culture and language. Christians and Jews that did not accept Islam lost the status of full-citizenship in their respective nations. They were reduced to the status of "Dhimmitude," "protectees" or wards of the Muslims. In return for this protection, they were expected to pay "the Jizya" (Poll tax).

The Pact of Omar[7]

Christians and Jews were also subjected to a long list of humiliating and degrading rules included in what is known as "the Pact of Omar." They were forced to sign a document, authored by Omar, agreeing to the following regulations and prohibitions.

- We shall not build new monasteries, churches, convents or monks' cells in our cities or in Muslim neighborhoods. Should any of these fall into ruins, we shall not repair, by day or night, those in our own neighborhoods or those situated in the quarters of the Muslims.
- We shall keep our gates wide open for passersby and travelers. All Muslims that pass our way are to be given board and lodging for as long as three days.
- We shall not hide any spy from the Muslims or give them sanctuary in our churches or shelter them in our homes.

- We shall not proclaim our religion publicly nor attempt to convert anyone to it. We shall not forbid any of our kin from entering Islam if they desire to do so.
- We shall show respect toward Muslims. If they wish to sit, we shall rise from our seats.
- We shall not seek to resemble Muslims by imitating any of their garments, turbans, footwear or parting of the hair. We shall not imitate their way of speech.
- We shall not mount on saddles, gird ourselves with swords, bear any kind of arms or conceal weapons on our bodies.
- We shall not engrave Arabic inscriptions on our seals.
- We shall not sell fermented drinks.
- We identify ourselves as non-Muslims by clipping the fronts of our heads.
- We shall always dress in the same manner wherever we go and we shall bind the zunar, identifying us as non-Muslims, around our waists.
- We shall not display our crosses or our books on the roads or in the markets of the Muslims. We shall use only clappers very softly in our churches. We shall not raise our voices in mourning when following our dead. We shall not shine lights on any of the roads of the Muslims or in their markets. We shall not bury our dead near the Muslims.
- We shall not take slaves who have been allotted to Muslims.
- We shall not build houses of taller elevation than the houses of Muslims.
- We accept these conditions for ourselves and for the people of our community, and in return we shall receive safe-conduct.
- If we in any way violate these regulations, for which we ourselves stand surety, we forfeit our covenant [dhimma] status and shall become liable to the penalties for contumacy and sedition.

Islam in Modern History

Nine hundred years after the first wave of Islamization, a second powerful wave took place, in the seventeenth century. The Ottoman Empire's Muslim Turks attempted to expand their rule into Europe. They captured Greece, Yugoslavia, Bulgaria, and parts of Romania and Hungary. By 1683, they had reached the gates of Vienna. However, once again, and against all odds, the Western forces were able, miraculously, to repel them[8].

Following this second failed attempt, to conquer Europe, Islam fell into a state of depression. In 1856, the Western countries pressured the Ottoman Empire to stop collecting the Jizya tax from Christians and Jews living in the Islamic world. The dhimmitude status was officially abolished; however, many of its provisions against Christians and Jews lingered on in the Islamic world. To this day, discrimination, and, at times, flagrant State-sanctioned persecutions against Christians and Jews run rampant in many Islamic countries.

A new Islamic awakening began taking place in the 20th Century[9]. It was not spawned by military might or the forced occupation of lands. Undoubtedly, in modern history, the driving force behind the new revival and acceptance of Islam was the discovery of vast reserves of oil in the Arab and Islamic countries. Oil became a strong weapon to advance the global influence of the Islamic oil-producing nations. Suddenly it became politically incorrect to criticize Islam or Muslims. Most importantly, with this new sword in hand, Muslims now have the means to finance their call to convert the world to Islam.

Now, in the 21st Century, Muslim advocates sense that they have the upper hand and therefore are becoming increasingly more aggressive in the West. They boast about being able to convert some 6-8 million people in the United States alone. Muslims challenge the historical fact that Islam has been spread by the sword. When speaking about their new converts they say, "Where is the sword? Nobody is using a sword against these people. They are coming into Islam on their own accord!"

In reality, the number of Muslims in the United States and the growth rate of Islam in America have been extremely exaggerated. Islamic activists inflate the figures by including Christians of Middle Eastern origin in the numbers cited as the United States Muslim population. The truth is, about 80% of the Arabic speaking people in America are actually affiliated with Christian denominations. The motive behind the exaggeration is to gain more political clout. A survey conducted by Tom W. Smith of the National Opinion Research Center in Chicago concluded that Muslim population figures ranged between 1.4 million and 2.8 million. The majority of these did not come through conversion but through immigration and procreation. In 1990, the *National Survey of Religious Identification* conducted a study. It was followed-up in 2001 by a study of the *American Survey of Religious Identification*. These studies demonstrated that Islam is by no means the fastest growing religion in America. Whether it is, by conversion, immigration, or procreation, it is being surpassed by a number of other religious groups.

Religion	1990 Est. Adult Population	2001 Est. Adult Population	%Of Change 1990 - 2001
Deist	6,000	49,000	+ 717%
Sikhism	13,000	57,000	+ 338%
Hinduism	227,000	766,000	+ 237%
Islam	527,000	1,104,000	+ 109%

It is undeniable, however, that Islam is seriously advancing in the West. This is mainly attributed to Islam's capacity to wield influence through its new sword of oil. The newly acquired wealth is currently being used in Western democracies in a manner that gives Islam a distinct economic advantage over Christianity.

With these factors in mind, it should be no surprise that Islam is growing in the West. In addition, unquestionably the Muslim activists of modern times are smarter and use more sophisticated tactics than those of ancient times. The days of the primitive methods that were used to conquer the known world, between the 7th – 17th centuries, are over. Islam now applies carefully studied and sophisticatedly executed methods. They define their targets, and decide on the best strategies to reach them. For example, a large army of Islamic activists are assigned for working among **prisoners**. They know that they can easily attract people who have issues with society. **Young women** are reached through love and marriage. With our **African-American citizens** the race card is used. Some were deceived into believing that Mohammed was black, that Islam was birthed on the African continent, and that they were Muslims before they were bought into slavery. To **the needy**, they use money. For **most people,** they polish Islam and present it in an attractively revised westernized form. The violent Quranic verses that were revealed in Medina are carefully excluded[10]. The peaceful verses of the Meccan era are emphasized. The fact is, according to Islamic theology, the early peaceful verses that were written in Mecca are nullified (abrogated), and replaced by the later verses that were written in Medina.

To **the religious establishment** they claim compatibility with the Judeo-Christian faith. They cite belief in Moses, Jesus, and the Virgin Mary. They concur with Christians and Jews on believing in God and the existence of

Heaven and Hell. Regardless of their boast that they have a lot in common with us, the fine print in Islamic teaching tells a different story.

Legally and politically they have the means to buy political influence and to retain high-powered teams of skilled lawyers. These experts find loopholes in our laws that enable Muslims to manipulate the system.

The Archbishop of Izmir, His Exc. Giuseppe Germano Bernandini, summed up the political dilemma of the West in relation to Islam by quoting an authoritative Muslim spokesman that he had encountered during an Islamic-Christian dialogue meeting. The man calmly stated with assurance, *"Thanks to your democratic laws we will invade you; thanks to our religious laws we will dominate you."*

In Conclusion, Islam is well on the road to becoming a major spiritual/political influence in the New World. It is imperative that we do not lose sight of the fact that its ultimate goal is to rule the world. It is patient enough, and sufficiently financed, to accomplish its goal, one country at a time. Muslim advocates are working fervently to convert America to Islam and they are gaining ground every day.

There is a thought that often wakes me at night: **The Muslims were able to conquer most of the known world in the 7th century with their limited and primitive means. What will happen to the world, if America becomes a Muslim country, and its might, wealth, technology, and resources fall into the hands of the Muslims? If this occurs, the New World will look like the old world. Time will lapse, and revert back to the 7th century and the New World's civilization will be reduced to a big barren Sahara.**

Chapter Three

ISLAM'S WEAPONS FOR THE ISLAMIZATION OF AMERICA

THE FIRST WEAPON

LYING

Muslim advocates are presenting to the West, today, a revised and polished version of Islam. It is not as much what they say but what they fail to say. This is called deception and lies by all measures and according to all faiths. But Islam sanctions this kind of deception as long as it is used for furthering the cause of Allah. To understand this, we need to study the subject of sanctioned lies in Islam.

Like most religions, Islam in general, forbids lying. The Quran says, "*Truly Allah guides not one who transgresses and lies."* Surah 40:28. In the Hadith, Mohammed was also quoted as saying, *"Be honest because honesty leads to goodness, and goodness leads to Paradise. Beware of falsehood because it leads to immorality, and immorality leads to Hell."*

However, unlike most religions, within Islam there are provisions under which lying is not simply tolerated, but actually encouraged. The book "The spirit of Islam," by the Muslim scholar, Afif A. Tabbarah was written to promote Islam[1]. On page 247, Tabbarah stated: "Lying is not always bad, to be sure; there are times when telling a lie is more profitable and better for the general welfare, and for the settlement of conciliation among people, than telling the truth. To this effect, the Prophet says: *He is not a false person who (through lies) settles conciliation among people, supports good or says what is good."*

In exploring this puzzling duplicity within Islam, we will examine first some examples from recent and ancient Islamic history. These examples demonstrate that lying is a common policy amongst Islamic clerics and statesmen.

In June of 1967 Egypt was defeated by Israel and lost the Sinai Peninsula during the "Six Day War." Subsequently, Egypt's primary focus became to regain the lost territory. President Nasser, and then, President Sadat, adopted the motto: "No voice should rise over the voice of **The Battle.**" The soldiers who have been drafted in 1967 were kept in service and remained on high alert in the expectation that at any day "the battle" would ensue. Nonetheless, years passed and Egypt's people became disgruntled with the political hype and the "no peace, and no war" status. In 1972 Sadat proclaimed with finality that it was to be the year for the long anticipated battle. Throughout the year he swore, *"I swear to you by my honor that this year will not pass by, before we launch The Battle."* People believed him because he was staking his reputation and honor through an oath. To everyone's amazement the year passed without a single shot being fired. As a result many, inside and outside Egypt, began to dismiss him as a "hot air bluff." This opinion was confirmed in the following year of 1973. He made no further mention of his oath about the battle. Many of the draftees were released and numerous officers were given vacation furloughs. Then without warning, in October of 1973, he launched the attack and what was known as the Yom Kippur war began.

As a military commander, President Sadat was expected to use the element of surprise to trick the enemy. As a devout Muslim, he was not the least bit concerned about his un-kept oath. He understood that the history and teachings of Islam would exempt him from spiritual accountability if he used lies as a foundation for a strategic military maneuver.

This point is proven by many incidences in the life of Mohammed. He often lied and instructed his followers to do the same. He rationalized that the prospect of success in missions to extend Islam's influence overrode Allah's initial prohibitions against lying. A good example of sanctioned lying is the account of the assassination of Kaab Ibn al-Ashraf, a member of the Jewish tribe, Banu al-Nudair[2]. It had been reported that Kaab had shown support for the Quraishites in their battle against Mohammed. This was compounded by another report that infuriated Mohammed. It was alleged that Kaab had recited amorous poetry to Muslim women. Mohammed asked for volunteers to rid him of Kaab Ibn al-Ashraf. As Mohammed put it, Kaab had "Harmed Allah and His Apostle." At that time Kaab Ibn al-Ashraf and his tribe were strong, so it was not easy for a stranger to infiltrate and execute the task. A Muslim man, by the name of Ibn Muslima, volunteered for the murderous project, on the condition that Mohammed would allow him to lie. With

Mohammed's consent, Ibn Muslima went to Kaab and told him fabricated stories that reflected discontent about Mohammed's leadership. When he had gained Kaab's trust he lured him away from his house one night and murdered him in a remote area under cover of darkness.

A similar example can be found in the story of killing Shaaban Ibn Khalid al-Hazly[3]. It was rumored that Shaaban was gathering an army to wage war on Mohammed. Mohammed retaliated by ordering Abdullah Ibn Anis to kill Shaaban. Again, the would-be killer asked the prophet's permission to lie. Mohammed agreed and then ordered the killer to lie by stating that he was a member of the Khazaa clan. When Shaaban saw Abdullah coming, he asked him, "From what tribe are you?" Abdullah answered, "From Khazaa." Abdullah then added, "I have heard that you are gathering an army to fight Mohammed and I came to join you." Abdullah started walking with Shaaban telling him how Mohammed came to them with the heretical teachings of Islam, and complained how Mohammed badmouthed the Arab patriarchs and ruined the Arabs' dreams. They continued in conversation until they arrived at Shaaban's tent. Shaaban's companions departed and Shaaban invited Abdullah to come inside and rest. Abdullah sat there until the atmosphere was quiet and he sensed that everyone was asleep. Abdullah severed Shaaban's head and carried it to Mohammed as a trophy. When Mohammed sighted Abdullah, he jubilantly shouted, "Your face has prospered (Aflaha al- wajho)." Abdullah returned the greeting by saying, "It is your face, Apostle of Allah, that has prospered. (Aflaha wajhoka, ya rasoul Allah)."

Provisions for lying in Islam
Most Muslims are familiar with the principles of Islam that will justify lying in situations where they sense the need to do so[4]. Among these are:
- War is deception.

- Necessities justify the forbidden.
- If faced by two evils, choose the lesser of the two.

These principles are derived from passages found in the Quran and the Hadith.

In the Quran, Allah, allegedly, says:
*"Allah will not call you to account for what is **futile in your oaths**, but He will call you to account for your deliberate oaths: for expiation, feed ten indigent persons, on a scale of the average for the food of your families; or clothe them; or give a slave his freedom. If that is beyond your means, fast for three days. That is the expiation for the oaths ye have sworn. But keep to your oaths. Thus doth Allah make clear to you His signs, that ye may be grateful."*   Surah 5:89

*"Allah will not call you to account for **thoughtlessness (vain) in your oaths**, but for the intention in your hearts; and He is Oft-forgiving, Most Forbearing."*   Surah 2:225

*"Any one who, **after accepting faith in Allah, utters Unbelief**, except under compulsion, his heart remaining firm in Faith - but such as open their breast to Unbelief, on them is Wrath from Allah, and theirs will be a dreadful Penalty."*   Surah 16: 106

The noted Islamic commentator, Al-Tabary explained Surah 16:106 as a verse that had been revealed to Mohammed after he learned that **Ammar Ibn Yasser** was forced to deny his faith in Mohammed when kidnapped by the Banu Moghera tribe. Mohammed consoled Ammar by telling him, "If they turned, you turn." (Meaning: if they again capture you, you are allowed to deny me again.)

These and similar passages from the Quran clearly reveal that Muslims can lie while under oath and can

even falsely deny faith in Allah, as long as they maintain the profession of faith in their hearts.

In the Hadith, Mohammed emphasizes the same concept.
From "Ehiaa Oloum al-Din," by the famous Islamic scholar al-Ghazali[5], Vol. 3: PP. 284 - 287:
One of Mohammed's daughters, Umm Kalthoum, testified that she had never heard the Apostle of Allah condone lying, except in these three situations:
1- For reconciliation among people
2- In war
3- Amongst spouses, to keep peace in the family

One passage from the Hadith quotes Mohammed as saying: "*The sons of Adam are accountable for all lies except those uttered to help bring reconciliation between Muslims.*"

Another says, "*Aba Kahl, reconcile among people* (Meaning even through lying)."

The following quote demonstrates the broadness of situations in which the prophet permitted lying. "The sons of Adam are accountable for all lies with these exceptions: During war because war is deception, to reconcile among two quarreling men, and for a man to appease his wife."

The principle of Al-Takeyya

The word "Takeyya" means "prevention" or "guarding against." The principle of Al-Takeyya conveys the understanding that Muslims are permitted to lie as a preventive measure to guard against anticipated harm to one's self or to fellow Muslims[6]. This principle gives Muslims the liberty to lie under circumstances that they perceive as life threatening. They can even deny the faith, if they do not mean it in their hearts. Al-Takeyya is based on the following Quranic verse:

"Let not the believers take for friends or helpers Unbelievers rather than believers: if any do that, in nothing will there be help from Allah: **except by way of precaution (prevention), that ye may Guard yourselves from them (prevent them from harming you***.) But Allah cautions you (To remember) Himself; for the final goal is to Allah."*   Surah 3: 28

According to this verse a Muslim can pretend to befriend infidels (in violation of the teachings of Islam) and display adherence with their unbelief to prevent them from harming him.

Under the concept of Al-Takeyya and short of killing another human being, if under the threat of force, it is legitimate for Muslims to act contrary to their faith. The following actions are acceptable[7]:
- Drink wine, abandon prayers, and skip fasting during Ramadan.
- Renounce belief in Allah.
- Kneel in homage to a deity other than Allah.
- Utter insincere oaths.

The implications of the principle of Al-Takeyya

Unfortunately, when dealing with Muslims, one must keep in mind that Muslims can communicate something with apparent sincerity, when in reality they may have just the opposite agenda in their hearts. Bluntly stated, Islam permits Muslims to lie anytime that they perceive that their own well-being, or that of Islam, is threatened.

In the sphere of international politics, the question is: Can Muslim countries be trusted to keep their end of the agreements that they sign with non-Muslim nations? It is a known Islamic practice, that when Muslims are weak they can agree with almost anything. Once they become strong, they can negate what they formerly vowed.

The principle of sanctioning lying for the cause of Islam bears grave implications in matters relating to the spread of the religion of Islam in the West. Muslim activists employ deceptive tactics in their attempts to polish Islam's image and make it more attractive to prospective converts. They carefully try to avoid, obscure, and omit mentioning any of the negative Islamic texts and teachings.

An example of Islamic deception is that Muslim activists always quote the passages of the Quran from the early part of Mohammed's ministry while living in Mecca. These texts are peaceful and exemplify tolerance toward those who are not followers of Islam. All the while, they are fully aware that these passages were abrogated (cancelled and replaced) by passages that came after he migrated to Medina. The replacement verses reflect prejudice, intolerance, and endorse violence upon unbelievers.

In conclusion, it is imperative to understand that Muslim leaders can use this loophole in their religion to absolve themselves from any permanent commitment. It is also important to know that what Muslim activists say to spread Islam may not always be the whole truth. When dealing with Muslims, what they _say_ is not the issue. The real issue is what they actually _mean_ in their hearts.

THE SECOND WEAPON

SEX

Sex has always been an important part in the make-up of Arab men. Arab men used to boast about two major abilities: the ability to fight and the ability to mate.

This is likely the reason that the early Arab Muslims honored their Apostle, Mohammed, by attributing him with super-human sexual strength. The Hadith says that Mohammed was given the sexual strength of 30 men. The legend is that he was able to engage in sexual relations with all 11 of his wives in a single hour round, during the day and the night:

*"Anas said, the prophet used to visit all his wives in **an hour round**, during the day and night and they were eleven in number. I asked Anas, had the prophet the strength for it? Anas replied: We used to say that the prophet was given the strength of thirty men."*

Al-Bukhari Vol. 1:268

Sex in Islamic Teaching
When Islam came into existence in Arabia in the 7th century, it was natural that it would reflect this reality and address this issue. The Quran and the Hadith, as well as

the teachings of the various Islamic schools of thought, deal in great detail with the important subject of sex. Mohammed, the prophet of Islam, was quoted as saying, *"mating (Nikah in Arabic) is my tradition; he that follows my tradition is of me."* Some counted more than 10,613 times where the word *"Nikah"* was mentioned in the Quran and Hadith. The word has been translated as "marriage" in English in many translations of the Quran and Hadith. But it actually refers to the physical part of the relationship in marriage.[1]

Marriage, sexual intimacy, adultery, divorce, etc, have all been regulated by Allah in the Quran and by His Apostle in the Hadith. Some of these regulations is that a Muslim man may marry 4 wives at a time. A Muslim husband is permitted to divorce any or all of his wives and remarry other women. The only condition is that he keeps no more than the four allowable wives and that he treats them equally. Mohammed, on the other hand, was given extra privileges; he was allowed an unlimited number of wives.

Islam specifies that the main role of the wife in marriage is to satisfy her husband's sexual desires[2].

In the Hadith: *"The prophet said: If a husband calls his wife to his bed and she refuses, and causes him to sleep with anger, the angels will curse her till the morning!"*

The Quran portrays a wife as a sex object in the marriage relationship. Her role is likened to a field that a husband ploughs, *"when or how"* he chooses.
"Your wives are as **a tilth** *unto you, so approach your tilth* **when or how you do**. " Surah 2:223

Abu Hanifa School of Islamic jurisdiction stipulates that the right of sexual pleasure belongs to the man, so the man has the right to force his wife to gratify him sexually.

The wife, on the other hand, doesn't have the same right over her husband.

In a Hadith (Mohammed's saying) Mohammed was quoted as saying that when a wife refuses to please her husband, the husband's future wives (hurries) in Paradise would rebuke her saying, *"Do not give him trouble. May Allah destroy you, he is only a passing guest with you and it is very near that he will soon leave you to come to us."* (Hadith # 2014 narrated by al-Termizy and Ibn Mageh)

Furthermore, Islam teaches that the way a wife treats her husband could be the factor which determines her destiny in eternity. Mohammed once said to a woman *"Watch how you treat your husband for he is your Paradise or your Hell."* (Al-Seiouty)

All Islamic schools of thought stipulate that a wife's dowry and her daily maintenance (wages) depend on her willingness to be available to her husband for sex. In other words, the wife is **paid** to please her husband sexually.
"Seeing that ye derive benefit (pleasure) from them (women), give them their dowers (wages) as prescribed."   Surah 4:24

This concept goes along the concept of "*marriage for pleasure.*" It is sometimes called "*contracted marriage*" or "*temporary marriage.*" This practice simply allows Muslim men to marry for a short time to satisfy their own desires for pleasure. Such marriages can last for hours or days, after which the marriage is automatically absolved. In return for sexual pleasures, the man pays the woman an agreed upon sum of money. Mohammed sanctioned this custom during times of war when men were away from home. Omar, the second Caliph, later abolished it. However, the Shiites, and even some Sunnis, still cling to it. Obviously, it is nothing short of legitimized prostitution.

Islam presents the reward of sex in Paradise as an incentive to attract Arab men, to join Islam. It is promised as a reward for warriors that fight for its cause. To those who are killed for the sake of Islam, Allah promises a Paradise filled with sexual escapades. There, each Muslim man will have some 70 virgins available to him for sex every day. They are told that God will automatically restore their virginity after each sexual encounter. The Quran is silent in regards to any sexual rewards being promised to Muslim women.

"We have created (their Companions) of special creation. And made them virgin - pure (and undefiled), - Beloved (by nature), equal in age, For the Companions of the Right Hand."   Surah 56:35-38

The Quran describes Paradise as a place where young boys will also be available to satisfy the sexual desires of some Muslim men, according to Muslim scholars. While alive, Muslim men who have such urges are required to suppress them out of obedience to God.

"Round about them will serve, (devoted) to them, young male servants (handsome) as Pearls well-guarded."
                                              Surah 52: 24

Sex as a tool for spreading Islam
It is natural with Muslims obsession with sex that they use it in every possible way. One of the most effective tools in the hands of Muslim men to spread Islam in the West is marrying non-Muslim women. According to the statistics, in the United States alone, an estimated 10,000 Christian women marry Muslim men every year.

Islam allows Muslim men to marry women from people of the Book (Christians and Jews). Theoretically, the Christian or Jewish wife can still keep her religion while married to a Muslim. But practically, very few of those wives are able to keep their Christian or Jewish faiths. After it is too late, they realize that they have fallen into a trap from which there is no way out. Women who choose to keep their religions face an unbearable price tag. Leaving Islam will likely cost them their full rights as wives and mothers, including the custody of their children. In addition, should they survive their Muslim husbands; they often find that they have been cut from the inheritance due to them.

On the other hand, for Muslim men it is a win, win deal. The foremost benefit is that it adds more converts to Islam. In addition, it may provide them with the requirements they need for gaining a residency status in the United States. Meanwhile they can enjoy free sex and perhaps a means of financial support. I heard once the story of a Muslim man that was a law graduate. He could not find work in his native country, Egypt. He left Egypt and over the next 30 years spent time in South America, the UK, and Europe. During his travels he married 9 different women. At the end, he died of cancer, but he was successful in the mission that every good Muslim has in mind, to spread Islam.

It is widely believed by Christians living in Islamic countries that there is another way in which the weapon of sex is being very effectively used. Islamic teaching does not allow Christian men to marry Muslim women. So, what happens? Young Muslim women try to sexually seduce Christian young men. Once the Christian man falls in love with the Muslim girl, he would be pressured to convert to Islam and marry her. Some of the enticements, that could add to the pressure, are the offer of free housing and good employment for the young Christian man if he converts. In countries where such things are in short supply, Christian young men, who are weak in the faith, can easily be tempted.

How Muslim men approach their victims in the West?

The bronze skin of Middle Eastern Muslim men looks great to many Western women. The physical attraction draws the young women to Muslim men. This is met by the equal attraction that Muslim men feel for Western women, especially the blond ones. They have a real knack for attracting them. It works like a strong two-way magnet.

In her book, <u>MARRIED TO MOHAMMED</u>[3], W.L.Cati, describes the reaction that she had to the Muslim man that she later married, after encountering him for the first time:

> *"There was something about him that I liked, and for some reason, I agreed to dance with him. And, he sure knew how to dance! He twirled me, spun me, threw me, and, literally swept me off my feet! For me, it was love at first sight."*

Besides being handsome, there are other qualities that a Muslim man might have that could impress a Western woman. He could be rich, intelligent, well educated and well mannered. So, what more can a woman ask for? Well, this most eligible bachelor is also a Muslim. The young woman must have heard stories about Islam and Muslims that could make her think twice before getting on this hazardous road. Friends may warn her to be careful. Concerned relatives may warn her that she is abandoning her Christian faith. To this, the Muslim man has a ready answer: *"There is no problem, you can keep your religion, and I will keep mine."* While it is true that as a Christian she is not required to convert to Islam, but is it practical not to do so?

In addition, the Muslim man might try to reduce the initial element of shock about the fact that the woman is marrying out of her faith. His tactic will be to try to break the dividing wall between the two religions by convincing her that Islam and Christianity are very similar. To do so, he may cite that Islam also believes in God, Jesus, the Virgin Mary, the Day of Judgment, and Heaven and Hell. He may even emphasize that Islam has an advantage over Christianity in that it is strictly a monotheistic religion. While it is true that Muslims believe in all of these, the question is, do they believe in them in the same way that Christians do? And, is it true that Christianity is not a monotheistic religion because it holds the belief in a triune God?

Muslim men might also try to convince their prospective victims about the virtues of Islam. They may talk about the modesty of Muslim women, explaining that they cover their bodies to protect their honor by reserving their physical beauty solely for their husbands. However, they would neglect to tell their victims that many Muslim women feel that this practice reduces them to ghost like figures, erasing their individual identities when in public. They boast that Islam guarantees a woman certain rights, such as a wife's right to own personal property separate from that of her husband. But it is not mentioned that a man's wealth is also entirely his own and that his wife doesn't have an equal share in it. They may talk about a woman's financial security under Islam, as a husband is responsible for the support of his wife. But it is not mentioned that a Muslim wife is completely dependent on her husband and that in cases of divorce, or his death, she risks losing all support.

A Christian woman that has been abused in the past would probably be reminded that it was her *"Christian"* ex-husband, or ex-boyfriend, that was responsible for it. However, it would not be mentioned that this has nothing to do with Christianity. Actually it has to do with the lack of Christian behavior. The fact is good people and bad people can be found among followers of all religions. Islam is certainly not immune from abusers.

Facts about Islam usually hidden from Christian women

Marrying a Muslim is marrying Islam. When a Christian woman marries a Muslim, the woman is initially allowed to practice Christianity. That is until time passes and the romance begins to fade. It is then that the Muslim husband will start to apply pressure, lies and trickery to force the Christian wife to convert to Islam.

We have previously mentioned sanctioned lying within Islam. Muslim men may lie by hiding certain parts of their religion when talking to prospective wives.

Christian women: Here are some facts that you won't be told, but will soon discover after marrying a Muslim man.

YOUR STATUS UNDER ISLAM

- **Men are superior to women.**
  *"And women shall have rights similar to the rights against them, according to what is equitable; but **men have a degree (of advantage) over them**."*
  Surah 2:228

- **Women have half the rights of men.**
  In court witness.
  *"And get two witnesses out of your own men, and if there are not two men, then a man and **two** women such as ye choose for witness."* Surah 2:282

70

And, in inheritance.
*"To the male a portion equal to that of **two** females"*
Surah 4:11

- **A wife is considered a possession.**
*"Fair in the eyes of men is the love of **things they covet**: Women and sons; Heaped-up hoards of gold and silver; horses branded (for blood and excellence); and (wealth of) cattle and well-tilled land. Such are the possessions of this world's life.."*
Surah 3:14

- **Women are unclean.**
If a Muslim **touches a woman**, even his own wife, before praying, he is considered **unclean** for prayer.
(Surah 4: 43)

- **Women must always veil themselves when outside of their homes.**
*"And say to the believing women that they should lower their gaze and guard their modesty; that they should **not display their beauty** and ornaments except what (must ordinarily) appear thereof; that they should draw their veils over their bosoms and not display their beauty."*
Surah 24: 31

WHAT MOHAMMED TAUGHT ABOUT WOMEN

- **Women are less intelligent than men and lack in their capacity to understand religion.**
*"I have not seen anyone more **deficient in intelligence and religion** than women."*
Al-Bukhari Vol. 2: 254

- **Women are a bad omen.**
*"**Bad omen is in the women**, the house and the horse."*
Al-Bukhari Vol. 7: 30

- **Women are harmful to men**
  *"After me I have not left any affliction more **harmful to men** than women."*   Al-Bukhari Vol. 7:33

YOUR MARRIAGE UNDER ISALM

- **Polygamy is allowed**
  *"Marry women of your choice, two, or three, or **four**."*
                                                        Surah 4:3

- **A man can divorce his wife by oral announcement; a wife doesn't have the same right. A man is allowed to divorce his wife twice and return her back.**
  *"A divorce is **permissible** twice"*   Surah 2:229

- **If a husband pronounces "divorce" on a wife three times, she cannot lawfully remarry him until she marries another man, has sex with him, and he divorces her.**
  *"...So if a husband divorces his wife he cannot after that, remarry her **until after she has married another husband**, and he has divorced her"*   Surah 2:230

- **A husband can beat his wife and abstain from sexual relations with her.**
  *"As to those women on whose part ye fear disloyalty and ill-conduct, **admonish them, refuse to share their beds, beat them...**"*   Surah 4:34

YOUR SEX LIFE

- **Islam considers a wife as a sex object.**
  *"Your wives are as **a tilth** (a field to be ploughed) unto you, so approach your tilth when or how ye will"*
                                                        Surah 2:223

YOUR CHILDREN

- **Your children must be raised as Muslims**.
  If he divorces you, he gets custody of the children, and you will not be able to see them again. The Sharia (Islamic Law) states that in mixed marriages, "the children will follow the better of the two religions of their parents." In your case, Islam will be considered the better of the two. The Quran states that Islam is the only true religion,
  "The (only) religion before Allah is Islam." Surah 3:19

- **Non-Muslims cannot act as protectors to Muslims.**
  *"O ye who believe; **take not for friends** (protectors) unbelievers rather than believers."* Surah 4:144

YOUR FUTURE

- Should you survive your Muslim husband's death, Islamic law will apply to any wealth that he has in an Islamic country. It dictates that a wife who has not converted to Islam receives nothing, and a wife who has converted receives very little. According to the Quran, a Muslim wife does not inherit all of her husband's wealth. If the husband dies and has no children, the wife receives only a fourth of his wealth. His surviving parents, brothers, uncles, etc. will receive the rest of the inheritance. If the deceased husband has children, the wife receives an eighth and the children receive the rest of the inheritance. A male child inherits double the portion of a female.
  *"In what ye leave, their (wives) share is **a fourth** if you leave no child; but if you leave a child, they (wives) get **an eighth**; after payment of legacies and debts."* Surah 4:12

WHAT DOES A CHRISTIAN WOMAN NEED TO DO BEFORE SHE TELLS A MUSLIM MAN "I DO."

Before a Christian woman commits herself in marriage to a Muslim, it is a good idea to examine the motives of all involved. While your motive may be love, his motive could be just to obtain a "Green Card" (a residency status.)

I know, they say, "love is blind." I hope, however, that this message will serve as an eye-opener for you Christian women who are thinking of marrying Muslim men.

A Christian woman may say that her husband-to-be is a non-practicing Muslim. But, let us not forget that Islam is more than a religion. It includes a complete legal code that Muslims and non-Muslims living in an Islamic State must follow. In a dispute, all he needs to do to get the upper hand is to travel to an Islamic country.

If Christian women are still in doubt about this, may I suggest that they see the movie, "Not without my daughter." It is based on the true life story of an American woman who married a Muslim. Other similar movies are: "Princess, Dreams of Trespass, and The Stoning of Soraya M." Viewing any one of these might be a life-saving experience. The lives saved will be that of the woman and those of her future children.

By doing this, Christian women will also be contributing to a great cause. They will be helping to spoil the Muslims' plan for invading the West.

"Be ye not unequally yoked together with unbelievers: for what fellowship hath righteousness with unrighteousness? And what communion hath light with darkness?"
2 Corinthians 6:14

THE THIRD WEAPON

RACE

The color of one's skin has suddenly become relevant to religion. Muslim activists have been using this sensitive and effective weapon especially among African American citizens. They have been trying to convince African American citizens that Islam is the religion of the Black man, that they were Muslim before they were brought to America, that Islam is African, and that Mohammed was Black.

Knowing that these are well thought-out falsifications, intended only to draw Blacks towards Islam, I felt compelled to set the facts straight. Nothing in this article is meant to lend approval to this racial approach. If we are to accept or reject Islam, it should be based on Islam's own merits, rather than color or origin.

Africa was not the cradle of Islam

Islam was born in the 7th century, in the Arabian Peninsula, which is part of the continent of Asia. Yellow Asia and Black Africa are separated by the Red Sea. Here, we are talking about two different continents and two different peoples.

Islam went to Africa relatively recently, and is not the predominant religion there. Africans were most likely either Christians or Animists at the time they were brought to America.

Christianity has been present in Africa since the first half of the first century. St. Mark, the writer of the Gospel of Mark was a North African Jew who preached the Gospel to Egypt. From there, Christianity spread all over North Africa, and to the south of Egypt's borders. The Eastern Church raised many Africans to the level of sainthood. Among these were the Egyptian, St. Moses the Black and St. Tekla Himanote the Ethiopian.

One of the teachers and prophets in the early church, Simeon, was believed to be an African from Niger, West Africa. (Acts 13:1)

Eastern Africa was converted to Christianity through the ministry of a cabinet member of Queen Candace of Ethiopia who was baptized by St. Philip, one of the seven deacons in the early church. (Acts 8:26 - 40)

Mohammed was not a Black Man

Mohammed was an Asian-Arab. You can't confuse an Asian-Arab with a Black-African. There are numerous evidences that Mohammed was actually White. The space limitation will allow us to mention only a few:

In Sahih Al Bukhary vol. 1 no. 63, we read
*"While we were sitting with the Prophet, a man came and said, 'Who amongst you is Mohammed?' We replied, 'This **white man** reclining on his arm.'"*

In volume 2 Hadith no. 122 refers to Mohammed as a "white person" and in vol. 2 Hadith no. 141 we are told that when Mohammed raised his arms, "the **whiteness** of his armpits became visible."

Mohammed Owned Black Slaves

Mohammed owned several black slaves. Ibn Qayyim al-Jawziyya relies heavily on the prophet's biographies written by great ancient scholars. Therefore, he is regarded by Muslims as an authority, a primary source and a leader among the students of Islamic religion. This scholar tells us in his book, "Zad al-Ma'ad" (part 1, pp. 114-116), the following:

"These are the names of Muhammad's male slaves: Yakan Abu Sharh, Aflah, 'Ubayd, Dhakwan, Tahman, Mirwan, Hunayn, Sanad, Fadala Yamamin, Anjasha al-Hadi, Mad'am, Karkara, Abu Rafi', Thawban, Ab Kabsha, Salih, Rabah, Yara Nubyan, Fadila, Waqid, Mabur, Abu Waqid, Kasam, Abu' Ayb, Abu Muwayhiba, Zayd Ibn Haritha, and also a black slave called Mahran."

Even in modern times, in Saudi Arabia the homeland of Islam, the common word for "Black" is "Abd" meaning slave.

What was Mohammed's position on freeing the slaves?

In one instance, a man freed a slave that he kept as a sexual partner. When Mohammed heard what happened, he auctioned the boy and sold him for 800 derhams to Naeem Ebn Abdullah Al- Nahham. (Sahih Moslem)

According to the Hadith, Mohammed said that the punishment for committing adultery is different between a free man, a free woman and a slave. The man is to be flogged one-hundred stripes and be exiled for one year. The free woman must be stoned to death. But the slave-woman (since she has a monetary value) will not be exiled or killed; she is to be flogged one-hundred stripes. If the violation is repeated, the slave-woman is to be sold.

(Sahih Al Bukhary vol. 8: 821 & 822)

Islam looks down on Blacks

Islam is a religion, whose sacred Scriptures contain explicit denigrating remarks about Black people. Mohammed referred to Blacks as "raisin heads".

(Sahih Al Bukhary vol. 1, no. 662 and vol. 9, no. 256)

Mohammed declared that a black woman was an evil omen. The Hadith says that Mohammed thought a dream of a black woman was an evil omen, signaling a coming epidemic of disease.   (Hadith vol. 9, nos. 162,163)

In another Hadith, Mohammed is quoted as saying that Blacks are, "pug-nosed slaves."

(Sahih Moslem vol. 9 pages 46 and 47)

Arab Muslims were the major traders in American Black slavery

African historian J.E. Inikori says that between the years 650 and 1900, Arab slave-traders drained Black Africa of 14.4 million people[1].

Dr. Harold Blackman, in his well-documented book "Ministry of Lies," wrote, "Between the years 650 and 1900, ten million or more Black Africans were carried by slavers either north across the Sahara or east over the Red Sea/Indian Ocean route. This trade was in the hands of Muslim merchants who made "Arab" synonymous with "slaver" and also supplied the Atlantic slave traffic." [2]

Yale professor David B. Davis says, "The Arabs and their Muslim allies were the first people to develop a specialized, long-distance slave trade from sub-Saharan Africa. They were also the first people to view Blacks as suited by nature for the lowest and most degrading form of bondage."[3]

Islam is not the Haven of Freedom and Equality

Even if we wrongly assume that Islam started in Africa and that its Prophet was a black man, this still would not in itself be a good reason for Blacks to adopt Islam. Nor would it be a good reason for Whites to adopt Islam just because Mohammed was white. We have to examine Islam itself.

I would not want to be a Muslim because Islam is anti freedom, which is one issue so close to the hearts and minds of African Americans, considering the inequities they have suffered in their past.

One thing Islam does not believe in is freedom of religion. If Islam takes over America there would not be a choice of religion. The Quran states:
*"If anyone desires a religion other than Islam, **never will it be accepted of him**; and in the hereafter he will be in the ranks of those who have lost."*   Surah 3:85

Many of the teachings of Islam are incompatible with progress. Neither are they compatible with human rights, civil rights or constitutional rights.

My fellow African-American:

Muslims do not care about your skin color, they are only using that to gain control over you. For if Muslims really care for Africans, why are African Muslims kidnapping their African Christian brothers these days in Sudan, butchering the weak and selling the healthy as slaves? (See State Dept. report: News Network International; May 26, 1993)

Consider, on the other hand, that Jesus Christ came to give us eternal life, where everybody stands equal in the sight of God. *"There is neither Jew nor Greek, there is neither bond nor free, there is neither male nor female; for ye are all one in Christ Jesus."*   Galatians 3:28

Muslim advocates use the race card, to conquer America from within, by dividing the citizens of this country. They attempt to bring bad memories of inequities that happened to Black citizens in the past to create a wedge between Blacks and Whites and to be able to spread their religion.

Of course, there was no justification for slavery; it was a horrible thing to happen to a human being. Unfortunately, it did happen, and for thousands of years, mostly to Blacks, but to other races as well. The Christian West was not the only guilty party for this sin. Arabs were the major traders of slavery throughout history.

It is also a fact, that Islamic nations did not free the slaves, the Christian West did. And, even in this 21[rst] century, Muslims in Africa still practice slavery. They kidnap black Christian women, boys and girls and sell them as slaves.

THE FOURTH WEAPON

MONEY

Before the discovery of oil in the Arabian Desert, in the 1930s, Saudi Arabia and Gulf States were mostly under-developed and extremely impoverished countries. Islamic countries used to help Saudi Arabia financially in the upkeep of the Kaaba. As an example, Egypt used to make a yearly donation to Saudi Arabia by providing a cover for the Kaaba. The caravan carrying the cover used to leave Upper Egypt in a big festival crossing the eastern desert until it reached the Red Sea, where it was taken by boat to Saudi Arabia and then to Mecca.

It was not until the second half of the 20th century that these countries started to force their place on the global map. Prior to World War II, these lands had been under French and British occupation. When the French and British pulled out, the United States moved in to fill the vacuum[1]. Both parties mutually accepted this. The newly rich countries felt threatened and needed protection from envious neighboring countries. On the other hand, the United States and the West were becoming increasingly dependent on their oil and needed to guarantee the uninterrupted flow of oil. Marshall Wyllie, a former envoy at the American embassy in Saudi Arabia, once summed up the American policy best: "We need their oil, and they need our protection."

However, Muslim zealots have never tolerated the presence of American troops and thousands of non-Muslim foreign experts in Saudi Arabia, the cradle of Islam. This comes from adherence to Mohammed's deathbed commandments when he said, *"Expel the pagans (non-Muslims) out of the Arabian peninsula,"* and, *"There should not be two religions left in Arabia."* These sayings have resulted in many violent acts, including the attack at Khober in Saudi Arabia. Bin Laden's al-Qaeda movement was originally established to protest his country's allowing non-Muslims on its soil.

How oil-money is used for the influence of Islam

The newly acquired wealth is currently used in Western democracies in a manner that gives Islam a distinct economic advantage over Christianity. Christians must depend on the sacrificial donations of their members to build and maintain churches, pay salaries and finance evangelism and benevolent outreaches. As a result of lack of funds, many Christian churches and organizations have to shut down and sell their buildings. Muslims who are using Petro-Dollars from the oil-rich Gulf and Saudi governments often purchase these defunct Christian properties. Muslim clerics, on the other hand, do not need to depend on donations to build mosques, pay their salaries and purchase airtime in the various broadcast Media. The financial aid they get from Islamic states enables them, also, to give generous assistance to needy people, who are potential converts to Islam. More seriously, it is reported that large sums of oil monies are covertly slipped into the hands of Muslim extremist organizations. Without any qualms of conscience, they finance terrorist attacks against non-Muslims and against moderate Muslims alike around the globe.

Oil and Dawa (proselytizing non-Muslims)

Before the newly found wealth, Islam around the globe was in a state of depression. The weakening of the Ottoman Empire, in mid 19th century, and the growing strength of the Western countries, kept Islam dormant. [2]

A century later, the discovery of oil became a new lifeline pumping life into the sleeping giant. Islam, since then, has started rising again, gaining ground, using a new sword called "money." With billions of dollars in hand, Muslims, especially the Saudis, now do not lack the funds to finance the Islamic movement around the globe. Using money to attract people to Islam is a concept deeply entrenched in the Islamic teachings. The Quran says: *"Alms are for the poor and the needy, and those employed to administer the (funds); (and) **for those whose hearts have been reconciled.** (to Truth)"* Surah 9:60. (The verse could also apply to **those whose hearts you want to reconcile**)

Soon, the influence of the money pouring from oil producing countries could be felt both inside and outside the Islamic world. In Arab countries, during the sixties, seventies and eighties, it was known that students were paid by Saudi funds to dress in the old fashioned Islamic tradition. You could then see a lot of male Muslim students growing beards and dressed in white Islamic robes and wearing slippers instead of shoes. Many female students started wearing veils. There were also reports that belly-dancers, singers, movie and theatre actresses were approached and offered money to take early retirement. In exchange these women were paid more than they could have expected to earn in a lifetime to abandon their jobs in the entertainment business and get veiled.

In March, 2002, a Saudi newspaper reported that Saudi Arabia was spending huge amounts of money throughout the non-Muslim world. The funds are being used to construct mosques and Islamic centers, support local Muslims and promote Islamic education. On top of these goals according to the newspaper, they are "spreading the word of Islam to every corner of the world." Saudi Arabia is using its massive oil wealth to engage in *dawa* for its Wahhabism, one of the most conservative forms of Islam. [3]

The *Barnabas Fund* reported that 210 Saudi-funded large mosques and Islamic centers have been built across the world's key cities. These include Washington D.C., New York, Los Angeles, London, Brussels, Geneva, Paris, Bonn, and Rome. In addition 1,500 smaller mosques, 202 colleges, and almost 2,000 Islamic schools have been built at other sites. Many Islamic organizations, such as the Australian Union of Islamic Councils are being funded by the same source. Prince Abdul Aziz Ibn Fahd spoke at the opening of a major new mosque and Islamic center in Edinburgh in 1998. He described the building of Islamic centers and mosques around the world as an "important part of the policy of Saudi Arabia which seeks to spread Islam and the message of wisdom and good counsel." [4]

According to the same report, it is believed that half of America's 1,200 mosques have been built, at least in part, with Saudi money. Earle H. Waugh, professor of religion at the University of Alberta, has said about Saudi Arabia's Wahhabi Islam, "they have a strong mission tradition, and they have used their money to export their ideology to America." Unfortunately, local authorities, being unaware of the expansionist agenda behind the new construction and these activities, have acted according to good community relations, and welcomed them. Some cities even donated the land on which such buildings were built.[5]

Among the Mosques built in the United States, an $11 million mosque was built on Manhattan's Upper East Side, with plans for a $29 million expansion. Near the University of Southern California Los Angeles campus, a 2,000-capacity mosque was built, costing $4 million. A steel-framed mosque, that was a work of art, costing around $8.5 million, was built in Culver City, California. All expenses for running the mosque have been provided by the Saudis. This includes a free package containing the Quran and Islamic books, which is presented to any visitor to the mosque. One of the most impressive mosques to date is the Islamic Center in Perrysburg, Ohio. Its mosque accommodates 1,200 people for services. The center opened in 1983 and boasts a membership that includes 22 different nationalities. Additional plans call for $40 million to be spent on an Islamic school, recreation center and other facilities. [6]

Even more disturbing is the Saudi funding for establishing numerous Islamic academic institutions to the secular colleges and universities of the West[7]. Islamic chairs have been set up at Harvard University, the University of California, the University of Southern California, the University of London and Moscow University, Saudi funds are providing scholarships for thousands of non-Muslims from the West to come and study at Islamic universities in Saudi Arabia[8]. It is assumed that the obvious aim of this is not merely to support academic education, but to introduce the Islamic faith to prospective converts.

Charitable donations made by Saudi Arabia are usually not only motivated by humanitarian concerns or alleviating the suffering. Their primary interests are the advancement of Islam and the winning of converts.

Upon the collapse of the USSR, while the Christian response was slow, Saudi Arabia responded quickly. Saudis established Islamic centers in the capitals of the six newly independent republics. Mosques were built in smaller cities. Millions of copies of the Quran were translated into local languages and airlifted to the region for free distribution.

The King Fahd Holy Quran Printing Complex in Medina has been printing hundreds of millions of copies of the Quran and audiocassette recordings of the readings of the Quran[9]. Many of these are distributed free of charge to mosques and Islamic centers around the world. Packages of these are also distributed to public and school libraries. One edition of the Quran that was donated to school libraries was challenged by a group of parents because they found denigrating comments about the Jews in the footnotes. Muslims rushed with a replacement that did not have such footnotes.

Mr. Hooper of CAIR Islamic organization confirmed in an interview that a Saudi billionaire, Prince Alwaleed bin Talal bin Abdul Aziz al Saud, donated $500,000 to CAIR for the educational push. "I think most of it is going for the library project," Mr. Hooper said. The report about the Saudi money prompted conservative activist Paul Weyrich, chairman of the Free Congress Foundation, to say that while libraries have intellectual freedom, the library packages "present a highly misleading view of Islam, spray-painting over the religion's long history of animosity to Western values." He called for the American Library Association to issue a statement on the problems with stocking a one-sided view of Islam and urged the use of materials written by his foundation's staff.

Oil and promoting the Islamic Agenda

According to Dateline, Cairo, January 26, 1996, Libyan dictator Moammar Gaddafi pledged $1 billion to influence American minorities in that year of presidential election. The pledge was made while the Nation of Islam's leader,

Louis Farrakhan, was visiting Libya, according to JANA, the Libyan government news agency. JANA quoted Gaddafi as saying, *"Our confrontation with America used to be like confronting a fortress from outside. Today we have found a loophole to enter the fortress and to confront it from within."*[10]

In his second stop Mr. Farrakhan went to Sudan to give support to a government that has been engaged in slave trading Black Christian citizens in the south. From there, he went to Iran to join the Iranian leaders in celebrating their 1979 revolution which included the seizure of the American embassy and the taking of American hostages. In Tehran, Mr. Farrakhan was quoted as telling the Tehran newspaper, *Kayhan,* "You can quote me: God will destroy America at the hands of Muslims." For once Mr. Farrakhan was partially correct; America may be destroyed at the hands of Muslims, but if it happens, God wouldn't have anything to do with it.

Oil funds are being used to influence elections in America. Senator Hillary Rodham Clinton, the former first lady, had to return $50,000 in political contributions received at a fund-raising event sponsored by a Muslim organization based in California. Mrs. Clinton later said she was offended by remarks attributed to members of the organization, the American Muslim Alliance. The group's president had been quoted as defending a United Nations resolution that he said allowed Palestinians to use armed forces against Israel. Other members of the organization were accused of making Anti-Semitic remarks.

About a month after the terrorist attack on September 11, 2001, a Saudi prince named Alwaleed bin Talal came to visit the site. There had been 15 Saudis involved in the terrorist attack out of the total of 19. Trying to improve his country's image, the Saudi prince presented Mayor Rudy Giuliani with a check for $10 million donation for the families of the victims. Soon afterward, the same prince made a speech justifying the terrorist attack. The prince was quoted as saying, "At times like this one, we must address some of the issues that led to such a criminal attack. I believe the government of the United States of America should reexamine its policies in the Middle East and adopt a more balanced stance toward the Palestinian cause." Mayor Giuliani was justified in returning the check to this kind of generous donor. The United States can do without the generosity of those that insult her.

Oil and Terrorism

A lot of money leaves Saudi Arabia from both the government and the private sectors. On the surface, these funds are directed to charitable causes. While some of these funds do go to charitable causes, knowledgeable banking sources report that in recent years a sizable amount of these funds has been diverted to Islamic extremist groups[11]. This includes those linked to Saudi-born fundamentalist, Osama bin Laden. Many wealthy Saudi and Persian Gulf businessmen are another source of financing for bin Laden's Al-Queda network. Many wealthy families in the region have members of their families with fundamentalist views and activities.

As I pen this section, it is reported that the Justice Department is investigating whether the Saudi government funneled money to two students who assisted two of the Sept. 11 terrorists. The FBI uncovered financial records showing payments to the family of Al-Bayoumi from a Washington bank account held in the name of the wife of the Saudi ambassador to the United States. Two of the terrorists met with Al-Bayoumi. American lawmakers strongly condemned the role Saudi Arabia played in the terrorist attacks. Sen. Charles Schumer of New York said, "Saudis have played a duplicitous game, in that they say to the terrorists, we will do everything you want, just leave us alone." Senator Lieberman said on CBS "Face the Nation" "For too many generations they have pacified and accommodated themselves to the most extreme, fanatical, violent elements of Islam, and those elements have now turned on us and the rest of the world." Added McCain: "The Saudi royal family has been engaged in a Faustian bargain for many years to keep themselves in power."

A 34-page report submitted to the United Nations in December 2002 concluded that despite a crackdown on terrorism financing after the September 11 attacks, Saudi Arabia still must dismantle a system that has permitted hundreds of millions of dollars to flow to Islamic extremists through businesses and charities. The investigator, Jean-Charles Brisard, said, "Al Qaeda was able to receive between $300 [million] and $500 [million] over the last 10 years from wealthy businessmen and bankers, whose fortunes represent about 20% of the Saudi GNP, through a web of charities and companies acting as fronts." [12]

The PLO archives have been made public by the Israeli army in the wake of its recent operation in the West Bank. The documents have confirmed that the Saudi government actively gives cash to a variety of terrorist organizations and showers the families of suicide bombers with money. This can no longer be seen as mere charity, but rather a premeditated incentive for murder. This means that the kingdom's suicide-killers of September 11, who butchered our civilians, were not so at odds with basic Saudi Arabia's policy after all. [13]

Oil and the War of Propaganda

Due to the fact that 15, out of the 19 terrorists of Sept 11, 2001, came from Saudi Arabia, the Saudi government has spent millions of dollars to improve its image among

Americans. In this quest, it is prepared to spend even more.[14]

The Saudis have hired several public relations firms and have spent millions of dollars, according to new Justice Department filings. These firms include prominent personalities known for their contacts among the Democrats, and others that have strong Republican credentials.[15]

An advisor to the Saudi government, and a lead figure in these efforts said that his government has adopted the techniques of an American political campaign to overhaul its image in this country. The strategy involves hiring a new publicity team accessible to the press, sending representatives on speaking tours, funding favorable research and polling the opinions of American citizens.[16]

Part of the strategy is running hundreds of paid advertisements via television, radio, newspapers and magazines. The advertisements emphasize Saudi Arabia's alliance with the United States and its commitment to fight terrorism.

In conclusion

These are just few examples of what Saudi Arabia has been doing in America with its oil-generated money. On a smaller scale, other rich Islamic Gulf states are doing the same thing. They have been given a free hand to influence American society with their culture, religion and interest. One can't help but wonder if these same countries would allow the American government and people to do the same inside their *Islamic* countries.

THE FIFTH WEAPON

TERROR

It happens almost daily, from Bali, to Moscow, to Tel Aviv, and it is a daily occurrence in Europe. Now it is beginning to be a serious threat to our peaceful way of life in the United States. The word is TERRORISM, and almost every time you hear or read about it, it is attached to the word "Islamic."

Islam: A religion of peace?

Muslim activists emphasize that Islam is a religion of peace. They say that "Islam" is derived from the Arabic word "Salam," meaning peace, while Islam, in fact, means "Surrender" (to the will of Allah).

To prove that Islam stands for peace, Muslims often quote certain verses out of the early period of the Quranic revelation. Here are some of them.

"Let there be no compulsion in religion."

Surah 2: 256

"And have patience with what they (opponents) say, and leave them with noble (dignity)."

Surah 73:10

However, what Muslim advocates deliberately fail to say is that the peaceful verses from the Meccan period have been abrogated (nullified) and replaced by the militant verses of the Medinan period. These verses were written after Mohammed moved to Medina, abandoned his peaceful approach and resorted to using the sword. As an example of the abrogation, 124 verses of the Quran that call for tolerance, peace, and patience have been canceled and replaced by this one single verse:

> *"Fight and slay the Pagans wherever ye find them, and seize them, beleaguer them, and lie in wait for them in every stratagem (of war.)"*
>
> Surah 9:5

Islamic violence around the world

The following are news items taken from newspapers in recent years:

November 28, 2002 - Mombassa, Kenya
"A statement attributed to al-Qaeda claimed responsibility for the car-bombing of an Israeli-owned hotel in Kenya and the attempt to shoot down an Israeli airliner in the same day. The statement called the attack a *"Ramadan Greeting"* to the Palestinian people."

October 14, 2002 - Bali, Indonesia
"In the tourist island of Bali, bombs were exploded by a Muslim group known as Jemiah Islami. The bombs were detonated in the "Sari Club and Hotel" and at the public "Kuta Beach," killing 200, mainly western tourists and wounding 500 that were mainly local Hindus. In poverty stricken Muslim Indonesia the island of Bali is an oasis of hope, generating 70% of the nation's tourism revenue."

September 11, 2001 - New York, USA
"Thousands of Americans are missing and presumed dead in the worst terrorist attack by Muslim extremists in the United States history. Two hijacked airliners on a suicide mission crashed into New York's Twin Towers, causing their collapse. A third crashed into the Pentagon, and a fourth went down in western Pennsylvania, its mission believed to have been thwarted by passengers."

October 12, 2000 - Aden, Yemen
"Muslim extremists crashed a small boat, loaded with explosives, into the Navy destroyer USS Cole, docked in the port of Aden, Yemen. The explosion blew a 40X40 hole in the ship killing 17 American sailors and injuring dozens of others."

August 7, 1998 - Kenya and Tanzania
"Bombs placed by Muslim extremists exploded at U.S embassies in Kenya and Tanzania, killing at least 224 people, including 12 Americans. Washington responded with cruise missile attacks on sites allegedly linked to Osama bin Laden."

November 17, 1997 - Luxor, Egypt
"Muslim militants marched into Southern Egypt's Temple of Hatshepsut and massacred 58 tourists. The incident was one of the deadliest acts of terrorism directed specifically at tourists."

June 25, 1996 - Khober, Saudi Arabia
"A Muslim extremist truck bomb exploded outside the Khobar Towers housing complex near Dhahran, Saudi Arabia. 19 U.S. Air Force personnel are killed and more than 500 Americans and Saudis are injured."

October 19, 1994 - Tel Aviv, Israel
"A powerful bomb, apparently placed by Islamic militants opposed to the Arab-Israeli peace negotiations, blew up a crowded bus during the morning rush hour in the heart of Tel Aviv, Israel. 22 people were killed and 48 were injured."

July 18, 1994 - Buenos Aires, Argentina
"A huge bomb placed by Muslim extremists exploded destroying a seven-story downtown building housing two Jewish groups in Buenos Aires, Argentina. At least 26 people were killed and 127 were injured."

February 26, 1993 – New York, USA
"A tremendous underground explosion rocks the 110-story twin towers of Manhattan's World Trade Center killing at least five people and injuring more than 1000. Tens of thousands of workers are sent fleeing for their lives down crowded smoke-filled stairs. Authorities believe that the explosion was caused by a bomb placed by Muslim extremists."

May 4, 1992 - Mansheit Nasser, Egypt
"13 Egyptian Christians were shot dead by Muslim fundamentalists in Mansheit Nasser, Egypt. Ten Christian farmers were ambushed and murdered while working in their fields. A Christian teacher was shot in the local school while teaching a class of ten-year olds. A Christian doctor was shot dead outside his home."

Silencing the opposition

Muslims have been taught not to question Allah and his Apostle. They are ordered to accept and practice their sayings regardless of how irrational they may sound. They were also taught to react violently toward anyone who questioned or criticized Allah or Mohammed.

Mohammed was a prime example of this to his followers; he had no tolerance for anyone who uttered the slightest insult about him. The poetess, *Asmaa bint Marwan,* was killed for uttering a few verses of poetry against Mohammed. A Muslim assassin, acting on Mohammed's orders, crept in at night to the women's bed, while her suckling baby was attached to her breast. The man plucked the baby from her breast and then plunged his sword into her abdomen. Another example was *Abu Afak*, an old man of 120 years of age, was murdered for composing poetry critical of the Prophet.

The essential problem is that the fruit of Mohammed's legacy exists today. As Muslims get deeper into Islam, they simply try to follow in the footsteps of their prime example by dealing in force against anything that they perceive as anti-Islam. Shaikh Abdul Aziz al-Alshaikh, the Grand Mufti of Saudi Arabia the highest official cleric in the country, issued a fatwa (sanction) which was published in the government's religious magazine "Al-Dawa," in May 11, 2000. The Fatwa was in an answer to a Muslim's question, "If there were websites on the Internet that are hostile to Islam, and broadcast immoral materials, is it permissible for me to send it viruses to disable these websites and destroy them?" Abdel Aziz answered, "If these websites are hostile to Islam and you could encounter its evilness with goodness, and respond to it, refute its falsehood, and show its void content; that would be the best option. But if you are unable to respond to it, and you wanted to destroy it and you have the ability to do so, its ok to destroy it because it is an evil website."

There are many examples of violent acts committed against intellectuals who in the course of their creative work stumbled into forbidden domains, and committed the unpardonable sin of speaking their mind against Islam or the prophet Mohammed.

- On November 26, 2002, the deputy governor of a largely Islamic state in northern Nigeria called on Muslims to kill the Nigerian writer of a newspaper article about the Miss World beauty pageant[1]. The article sparked deadly riots that killed about 215 and injured over 500 people. 4,500 lost their homes in reaction to the article. **Isioma Daniel**, a Lagos-based fashion writer, was commenting on Muslims objection to the beauty pageant and reportedly wrote that Mohammed would have approved of the pageant: "What would Mohammed think? In all honesty, he would probably have chosen a wife from among them." This comment was seen by Muslims as an insult to their prophet. A Muslim leader issued an edict, "If she (Daniel) is Muslim, she has no option except to die. But if she is a non-Muslim, the only way out for her is to convert to Islam." Daniel now is in hiding.

- On November 5, 2002, Professor **Hashem Aghajari**, was sentenced to death in Tehran[2]. He was charged for questioning the hard-line clergy's interpretation of the Quran. In a speech, Aghajari had said that the clerics' teachings on Islam were considered sacred simply because they were part of history, and he questioned why clerics were the only ones authorized to interpret Islam. Aghajari's speech provoked organized street rallies by hard-liners in several cities.

- On July 30, 2001, well-known Egyptian feminist writer, **Nawal Al-Saadawi**, appeared in court. A case had been filed against her in May, calling for a divorce from her husband, Sherif Hitata, in relation to comments she had made on religious issues[3]. The complaints against her were based on the *"Hisba" law.* It is an Islamic legal procedure that allows an individual to file complaints, on behalf of society, against another individual.

- In 1995, **Dr. Nasr Hamed Abu Zeid**, a university professor in Cairo, was faced with similar charges. On June 14, 1995, a Court of Appeal ruled that he had insulted the Islamic faith in his writings[4]. It ordered his wife to divorce him on the grounds that, as a Muslim, she should not remain married to an apostate. The Court of Cassation upheld the ruling in August of 1996. Dr. Nasr and his wife are currently living in exile in Europe and continue to challenge their forced divorce before a judicial appeals body in Egypt.

- On June 4, 1994, **Taslima Nasrin**, 32, a Bangladesh feminist and writer, fled her Dhaka apartment and went into hiding[5]. A warrant was issued for her arrest after a newspaper in India quoted her as saying that the Quran should be revised. She was accused of offending the religious sentiments of Muslims. Nasrin denied making such statement, saying that she had not called for a revision of the Quran, but of Islamic law, known as Sharia. Despite her denial and clarification, Muslims radicals intensified their campaign against her. A Muslim leader in Khulna, 30 miles south of Dhaka, offered $2,500 in cash for her assassination. The government finally charged her with "intent to deliberately and maliciously outrage the religious feelings of Muslims."

- In 1988 **Naguib Mahfouz** received his Nobel Prize for Literature for his novel, "Children of Gebelawi". Islamic fundamentalist later condemned the novel as blasphemous[6]. This caused an uproar akin to the later reaction against Salman Rushdie's, *Satanic Verses*. In 1994 the Nobel Prize laureate was stabbed in the neck with a kitchen knife. Two Egyptian Islamic militants were sentenced to death in 1995 for attempting to kill him. Upon questioning, the assailants admitted that they had never read the novel, and that they had acted upon a religious fatwa (edict) made by their leaders.

- In June 1992 a member of *Gamaa Islamiya* assassinated **Dr. Farag Fouda**[7], an Egyptian university professor, an intellectual, and a staunch advocate of secularism. His assassin confessed that he was motivated by a debate between Fouda, Ghazali and Hodeibi, and a statement made by a council of Azhar scholars calling Fouda "a follower of the non-religious current and extremely hostile to anything Islamic." He reported that he felt that the assassination was his duty for the fulfillment of Islamist objectives. Farag Fouda was the first to warn against the ideas of the Taliban and Al-Qaeda.

- In 1988, **Salman Rushdie**, an Anglo-Indian novelist received his Whitbread Award for his novel "*The Satanic Verses*." Later, the novel was criticized by Islamists around the world, banned in India and South Africa, and burned on the streets of Bradford, Yorkshire, UK. The Ayotollah Khomeini issued a fatwa (an edict) to execute the writer and the publisher of the book[8]. An aid to Khomeini offered a million-dollar reward for Rushdie's death. In 1990 Rushdie published an essay titled "*In Good Faith*" to appease his critics and issued an apology in which he reaffirmed his respect for Islam. However, Iranian clerics did not withdraw their death threat. In 1993 the publisher was wounded in an attack outside his house. Rushdie went into hiding. In 1997 the price on Rushdie's head was doubled. A few years later the highest Iranian state prosecutor, Morteza Moqtadale, renewed the death sentence. During this period of fatwa, violent protest broke out in India, Pakistan, and Egypt causing several deaths.

The items that I have mentioned are just a few examples out of thousands of terrorist attacks. They all have one element in common: they were all committed by Muslim extremists. While there are extremists in other groups who are capable of committing acts of violence, it seems that violence committed by Muslim extremists exceeds the violence of all other groups combined.

Why do Muslim extremists act this way?
Are Muslims acting this way because they are inherently inhuman, savage, and evil? Of course not; Muslims are ordinary people, just like anybody else. They are fathers, brothers and sons. They are doctors, engineers and lawyers. They are your co-workers, and your next-door neighbors. Only the Muslims who hold extremist views are capable of committing these acts of violence.

So, what goes on in their minds, causing them to act violently?
To understand this, one must understand an important and dangerous Islamic teaching called "Jihad" (Holy war). It is important to understand that not every Arab is a Muslim, not every Muslim is an Arab, and not every Muslim is an extremist. We are not trying to attack a group of people here; we are only exposing a teaching within a religion that could have a serious effect on all society.

It is also important to know that in exercising Jihad, Muslims may not think they are trying to maliciously hurt others, but rather they think that they are only obeying God's commandments. And, by doing so, they are assuring themselves of a place in Paradise.

Jihad (Holy War)

Jihad is one of many sacred duties Muslims perform. The word "Jihad" is an Arabic word, which means, "struggle." Jihad can mean the struggle within oneself to be a better Muslim, but it can also mean fighting in the name of Allah. In this sense Jihad is the struggle for the cause of spreading Islam, using all means available to Muslims including force. This kind of Jihad is often referred to as "Holy War."

In resorting to force, Muslims will not have any problem finding passages in the Quran (believed by Muslims to be Allah's word), and the Hadith (Mohammed's sayings), that not only condone violence, but demand it. Somebody counted the times the word "*kill*" and other words derived from it that appeared in the Quran and Hadith and found them to be about 24,400 times.

It is bad enough if a religion calls on adherents to kill themselves, but what right do they have to kill others? If Allah gives Muslims the right to kill, what kind of God is he that orders followers to kill innocent people on his behalf?

Jihad in the Quran
Allah orders Muslims in the Quran to terrorize non-Muslims on His behalf:
> "**Strike terror** (into the hearts of) the enemies of Allah and your enemies." Surah 8:60

"Fight (kill) them (non-Muslims), and Allah will punish (torment) them by your hands, cover them with shame." Surah 9:14

*"I will **instill terror** into the hearts of the unbelievers, smite ye above their necks and smite all their fingertips off them It is not ye who slew them; it was Allah."* Surah 8:12, 17

*"But when the forbidden months are past, **then fight and slay the Pagans** wherever ye find them, and seize them, beleaguer them, and lie in wait for them in every stratagem (of war); but if they repent, and establish regular prayers and practice regular charity, then open the way for them: for Allah is Oft-forgiving, Most Merciful."* Surah 9:5

*"**Fight (kill)** those who believe not in Allah, nor the Last Day, nor hold that forbidden which hath been forbidden by Allah and His Messenger, nor acknowledge the religion of Truth, (even if they are) of the People of the Book, until they pay the Jizya with willing submission, and feel themselves subdued."* Surah 9:29

Jihad in the "Hadith"

In the Hadith, Mohammed also urges Muslims to practice Jihad. Mohammed once was asked: "what is the best deed for the Muslim next to believing in Allah and His Apostle?" His answer was: *"To participate in Jihad in Allah's cause."*
Al Bukhari vol. 1:25

Mohammed was quoted as saying: *"I have been ordered **to fight** with the people till they say, none has the right to be worshipped but Allah."*
Al Bukhari vol. 4:196

Mohammed also said, "*the person who participates in (Holy Battles) in Allah's cause and nothing compels him to do so except belief in Allah and His Apostle, will be recompensed by Allah either with a reward, or booty (if he survives) or will be admitted to paradise (if he is killed).*"   Al Bukhari vol. 1:35

Mohammed's Example

When the prophet of Islam started preaching his new religion in Mecca, he was conciliatory to Christians and Jews. He told them: "*We believe in what has been sent down to us and sent down to you, **our God is the same as your God.***"   Surah 29:45

This attitude changed completely after he gained strength. Allah then allegedly told him to "***Fight People of the Book** (Christians and Jews), who do not accept the religion of the truth (Islam), until they pay tribute (penalty tax) by hand, being inferior.*"   Surah 9:29

Comparing Christians to the Jews, it seems that Mohammed hated the Jews more.   The Quran clearly states:
"***Strongest among men in enmity** to the believers wilt thou find **the Jews** and Pagans; and **nearest among them in love** to the believers wilt thou find those who say, "We are **Christians**": because amongst these are men devoted to learning and men who have renounced the world, and they are not arrogant.*"   Surah 5 : 82

During his lifetime, Mohammed devoted much of his efforts to get rid of the Jews. He stated. "*You (Jews) should know that the earth belongs to Allah and his apostle, and I want to expel you from this land (the Arabian Peninsula), so, if anyone owns property, he is permitted to sell it.*"   Al-Bukhari vol. 4:392

At that time, there were three Jewish tribes in Medina. Mohammed's men besieged two of them, the Bani Qaynqa and the Bani-al-Nudair tribes. Their access to food supplies was blocked until they surrendered on Mohammed's terms. His terms for their lives to be spared were that they had to deposit all their belongings at a certain place for distribution among Muslims and then emigrate from Medina[9].

The third tribe, Bani Qurayza, was not as lucky. During *the War of the Trench*, Abu Sofyan led a siege against Mohammed's forces. Afterward, it was alleged that Bani Qurayza agreed to provide help from within to Abu Sofyan's forces. The alleged help never materialized and the siege eventually ended. Nonetheless, Mohammed never forgave them for their willingness to help his enemies.

The Muslims turned against the Bani Qurayza tribe and blocked their streets for twenty-five days. Then the Jewish tribe expressed readiness to accept the surrender terms that had been afforded to the other two Jewish tribes. Their belongings were to be confiscated and they were to be granted safe conduct for their departure from the area[10].

Mohammed, however, would not consent to this. Instead he appointed as an arbiter Saad iben Moaz, a man who was known to be on bad terms with Bani Qurayza. Saad ruled that all Bani Qurayza's men should be beheaded, that the women and children should be sold as slaves and that all their property should be divided among the Muslims. Trenches were dug in the bazaar of Medina for disposal of the eight to nine hundred Jewish bodies whom Mohammed and his men had spent the night slaughtering. (See Ibn Hisham: The Prophet's biography; vol. 2 pages 240 & 241).[11]

In Conclusion:

These are historical facts that occurred 14 centuries ago. They represent a dangerous tendency for violence in the Muslim mentality. More serious is that Muslim fundamentalists are trying to repeat these acts of violence in this 21st century.

In doing so they are terrorizing individuals and governments as well. Islamic violent protests occur around the world whenever Islam is being criticized. As a result, governments around the globe have started to enact laws under the pretext of "hate crimes." These laws prosecute anyone who criticizes Islam or Muslims. The laws have, in fact, very little to do with hate crimes. They are designed only to appease Muslims, and quell their wrath, for the sake of peace and tranquility in society.

Nothing is mentioned about the criticism Christianity receives from Muslim religious leaders in the media of the Islamic world and of the West as well. But Christians are tolerant of criticism against their religion; no riots, nobody gets killed, and no buildings get burned. No wonder, nobody cares about hate crimes against Christians.

Once again we are being held hostage. One of the weapons that are being used to keep us as hostages is terror, and more terror.

Conclusion

Summary and Recommendations

Islam is not just a religion, and should not be treated only as one. Islam is a comprehensive way of life; social, political, economic as well as religious. In Islam there is no separation between Church and State; Islam teaches that it is a religion which must control the State.

Muslims' loyalty is, first and foremost, to their religion and the followers of their religion, the *"Umma"* (the body of Muslims). Mohammed was quoted as telling Muslims, *"Take the side of your (Muslim) brother whether he was right or wrong."*

Islam teaches that Muslims and non-Muslims belong to two different and opposing camps, Muslims belong to *Dar al-Islam* (the House of Islam) and the non-Muslims belong to *Dar al-Harb* (the House of War). As a result, Muslims are in a constant state of war with non-Muslims.

Islam's ultimate goal is **to rule the entire world**. If they are not doing it today, it is because they are not yet militarily strong enough. At one time, Muslims invaded and occupied most of the known world. Because they do not possess the military might to continue their mission, they are resorting now to alternative tactics. Among the weapons that Muslims use these days to spread their religion are: Lying, Sex, Race, Money and Terror. **If America's military power falls in the hands of Muslims, you can be sure that they *will* use it to subjugate the rest of the world to Islam.**

Now, what to do about it?

The Islamic invasion of America is real. We need to regard it as an emergency situation that requires the immediate attention of every American.

The Government

- It is true that clever men, anointed by the Holy Spirit for the task, authored our Bill of Rights and its Amendments to our Constitution. We now need keen legislative minds to lobby creative suggestions for updating the amendments. Our current Congressional representatives can be inspired to craft legislation that will protect us from our foes without violating the spirit of the Constitution. Even if it might ultimately require a Constitutional Convention, concerned Americans must begin to voice the necessity of this to their representatives.

- Resist any legislation that would empower tax-exempt religious organizations with increased abilities for political influence. The conservative Christian Right recently lobbied for laws that would permit them to use larger percentages of their funds for political purposes. This ploy is deceptive. It equally empowers Islam to use its vast resources to sway our politicians and to assert its agenda for religious dominance from Mosques.

- Our government would serve us well by enacting laws that would discourage excessive foreign funding for religious groups within the United States. The Saudis and other oil producing Islamic states are now funding the Islamization of America under the guise of charity to U.S. based Muslim institutions. In effect, petro-dollars are financing the demise of our way of life.

- We should call for a restriction on the number of visas granted to Islamic foreign nationals each year. We must demand that the Department of Homeland Security closely monitor those that currently hold educational and business visas. Those that are in visa violation should be instantly deported.

- **In dealing with Islamic countries, the United States government must insist on the principle of reciprocation**. A country such as Saudi Arabia must not be allowed to build thousands of mosques in the United States and the West, while not allowing the building of a single church on its soil. Furthermore, Muslim countries must not be allowed to send activists to our country to convert Americans to Islam while they don't allow Christian missionaries in their countries.

- **The government must, as soon as possible, employ specialized teams of scientists and technologists and entrust them with the single task of developing a new alternative source of energy other than oil. It is alarming to know that every time we pay for gas at the pump, we may be indirectly contributing to the Islamization of America. In addition, we can never be really free from the possibility of blackmail until we stop our dependency on Middle East oil.**

The Church

- Our faith, our people, our culture and our way of life are under attack. All of us as members of the Christian church must get on our knees in prayer and fasting for the deliverance of America from Islamization. *"Howbeit this kind goeth not out but by prayer and fasting."* Matthew 17:21

- We need to pray that our national, state, and local police investigative agencies will uncover the plots of the multitudes of terror cell members and their supporters that are living amongst us. In faith, rather than fear, intermittently ask the Lord to protect our children, family, and friends from potential harm by homicidal bombers[1].

- Our churches and Christian organizations need to get back to the basics of the Christian faith. Jesus said, "I am the way, the truth and the life." John 14:6. **We need to be clear on the fact that all religions are not equal, and all do not lead to eternal life**. The church must equip members with the spiritual weapons to defend themselves against heresies and cults such as Islam. It is the responsibility of the church to teach its members the Christian doctrines that are often attacked by Muslims such as the Crucifixion of Jesus, the Triune God, and the authority and infallibility of the Bible. The basic differences between Christianity and Islam must be explained in a clear and unambiguous way.

- Pastors of our churches need to be careful about accepting invitations to interfaith meetings with Muslims. These are often simply Islamic ploys to win Christians' approval that our clergymen should not fall for. Their participation in what are called "dialogues" and "building bridges," with Muslims, gives Muslims the legitimacy and acceptance they badly need to spread their religion in American society.

- We thank God for the existing Christian prison ministries. We need to do more in this field. We must take prisons back from Islamic activists. It is of very serious consequences to have these thousands of prisoners, who already have issues with society, come out of prisons indoctrinated in an Islamic ideology that harbors enmity towards society and is prone to violence.

The Family

- It is not enough to provide a living for our children; Christian parents must protect their children spiritually from the influence of other teachings. The family must keep channels of communications open with their children and provide them with information regarding dangerous teachings such as Islam. Islamic beliefs must be explained to our children in clear terms. They must know that it is not a legitimate extension of Christianity. **It should be emphasized that as Christians, we do not believe that Islam can lead anyone to the eternal salvation of their souls.**

- Parents need to know whom our children are befriending. **If any of our daughters start to have relationships with Muslim men, it should be considered a serious situation that needs to be handled with prayer, wisdom and knowledgeable counsel.** All of the tragic implications of marriage to a Muslim must be explained to our daughters.

The Individual
- We first need to become informed about the subject by attending seminars and studying books, magazines and websites, etc.

- Then, we need to get the truth out. Each and every one of us has a role to perform. Some of us can write and some can make speeches, while others can financially support the cause or distribute tracts and literature. All efforts are needed and are important.

- We are eyes and ears for the authorities. We need to be vigilant as we carry on our daily lives. If we suspect any illegal or suspicious activities, we must immediately report them to the authorities. In doing so, we need to free ourselves from any prejudicial tendencies. We must understand that violence is not necessarily connected to a certain race or ethnic group. There are good, law-abiding and God-fearing people in every race and ethnic group. The opposite is also true.

In Conclusion
This book was not designed to convey a negative message. It is true that the dangers that surround us are enormous. But on a positive note, we need to know that the final victory is for the truth. This, however, should not absolve us from our responsibilities. We are the tools that God uses to carry out His plan. We, who in God's plan are witnesses to the threat of Islam, bear the responsibility to do what we can to challenge its growth. And, by God's grace and power, we will prevail.

A Muslim's Vision for America

How do Muslims envision America? What kind of change Muslims will enforce on all Americans should they have their way in Islamizing America?

Following are direct quotes of statements made by Imam (Muslim clergy) Abdullah Yasin in his pro-Islam book "Islamicizing America," published by James C. Winston, Nashville, Tennessee, 1996.

Mass conversion to Islam

"This (Islamicizing America) will not happen en masse until they begin, en masse, to accept Islamic leadership which is based only upon the Quran and Sunnah. Once this begins to happen, and I sincerely believe it will, we will find Americans accepting Islam from quarters we had not expected. Those 'existing' individual local and national groups of Muslims will all but pale into insignificance by the overwhelming numbers of prospective Muslims in American society who are only a hands breadth away from accepting Islam. Insha'Allah (God's willing)."

Allah is using natural disasters to humble America
"Allah can cause the earth to open and swallow any armed man or nation along with its weapons of war. Man and his missiles are no match for Allah's wrath. Man should take heed, for as I pen these very words Hurricane Andrew is pounding Florida and there is nothing man can do to prevent its destruction! Nothing!"

What does it mean to Islamize America?
"When we speak of Islamizing a society, we must necessarily mean changing the direction of its culture."
"The United States sorely needs the medical effects of Islam to save it from the disease of self-destruction."
"Unlimited freedom is destructive. Just look at American (Western) women. Trying to be men! Abandoning their God-given role of the mothers of society. These so-called liberated women are fighting against men; they are rebelling against God and challenging His authority to create!"

Playing the race card
"First, I must make it absolutely clear that the design-plan(s) I present are geared primarily, though not exclusively, toward the African-American in general and African-American Muslim in particular."
"The African-American knows he is somebody! But "who" Christianity has not taught him."
"Christianity was never intended to help him gain his freedom! He was not Christian when he came here! Can not today's African-American leadership see that this "religion" (Christianity) was only meant to be temporarily used as a surreptitious "survival tool"? Certainly his leadership can see that for the past two centuries it has all but failed him and the rest of the world?"
"Wake up Africans, this religion (Christianity) is killing you; worse it is a tool of your continual enslavement."

Islam is not a religion
"When speaking of religions, it should be emphasized that Islam is not a religion! Islam is a "way of life" and we must always look upon it as such. From this day on, we should never again refer to Islam as a religion.""

The Muslim's façade
"Especially when talking to non-Muslims, Muslims must learn how to be non-religious."

"The Trinity" is a pagan belief
"All the hocus-pocus must come from the side of confusion and uncertainty. That is one of the trappings of Christianity's "Trinity," Pagan belief.""

The entertainment and sport industries
"The entertainment industry and the sport industry have made millionaires out of many African-Americans. So what has it profited the masses? Nothing, but to lead them further astray. How many Bill Cosbys or Oprah Winfreys are there? Too, too few. How is all of their money being spent? Mostly by low moral, hell raising, big hat wearing and big car driving self indulgers."

Men's superiority over women
"Whether one likes it or not, this is man's world. And men are not going to be controlled by women and her role as a woman does not entitle her to a fifty percent share in universal sovereignty. Her soul is equal to man's, but her role is not!"
"Foolish people try to make men and women equal. They are not. Neither is equal to the other."

Women behind veil
"Instead of being out on a date, she (a woman) should be home or somewhere behind a veil if she didn't want to be raped."

A woman can not marry without a guardian

"According to the four Orthodox Islamic Schools of Law it is unlawful for a woman to marry without a guardian. However, the Hanifi School gives her a bit more independence, while the Prophetic tradition makes it clear that even in such a case the Ruler is in fact her guardian. And what must be realized in looking at this Hanifi viewpoint, is that the woman, in a land governed by this School of Law, is still surrounded by her Muslim family. and family is going to look after and protect its own from harm."

Polygyny (one man married to more than one wife) is the rule

"All-Mighty Allah has made polygyny lawful. Only a disbeliever would say it is unlawful. Neither I, you, the United States Government, nor the United Nations of the world can make unlawful that which Allah (SWT) has made lawful."

"A society which endorses monogamy only is going to be filled with licentiousness, lies, deceit, and unbridled deviant sexual attitudes. Look at western society."

Islam is the one that destroyed the Evil Empire

"With the demise of the Evil Empire, which was destroyed not by the west but by Islam through Afghanistan, these enemies are attempting, with relative success, to cast Islam into the void left behind."

When Islamic laws collide with United States laws

"There is only one primary law and it is Allah's law. All manmade laws must take a back seat to His law and if anyone says that Allah says in the Quran that you must follow or obey the law of the land in deference to Allah's law, ask the liar to show it to you. He can't, and he won't, because Allah would never give an order which even possibly leads to disbelief. For the law of this land approves of and orders many un-Islamic things."

Crime and Punishment

"For the benefit of many of our Muslim and non-Muslim readers, we list the following prescribed punishments for eight major crimes which are to be implemented in an Islamic State. They are:
1. Rebellion against the Khalifah (ruler)
   - Crucifixion, execution, or exile.
2. Apostasy from Islam
   -Execution by beheading.
3. Adultery
   -One hundred lashes and then stoning to death.
4. Fornication
   -One hundred lashes, then exile for one year.
5. Drinking alcohol/ intoxication
   -Eighty lashes.
6. Theft/denial of a borrowed item
   - Amputation of the right hand.
7. Slander by accusing someone of adultery
   - Eighty lashes
8. Murder
   - (Depends on the circumstances)".

Pray, or get beaten

"The Prophet Mohammed (PBUH) is reported to have said: Command your children to pray when they become seven years old, and beat them for it when they become ten years old."

All members of the family pay for the mistake of one

"(When somebody kills another person), his family should have to pay blood money to the family of the victim. Yes, all immediate family members (grandparents, parents, brothers, sisters, uncles and aunts) will have to collectively pay this debt on behalf of the executed murderer."

Banking, interest and Insurance not allowed
"Banking, interest, and insurance are so closely related in the present circumstances that they, more often than not, determine the state of the economy. Interest, pure and simple, is unlawful and is a major cause of the world's moral and economic problems."

Buy a home, pay in cash
"Why should one buy a one hundred thousand dollar home and be forced to pay a lending institution nearly a half million dollars over the course of twenty-five to thirty years? This is financial slavery! Insanity! "

Back to the 7th century
"What must be kept in mind is that 20th/21st century technology must never supplant 7th century morality.

The Bottom Line:
If Islam gets its way in America, it will take America back to the 7th century way of life.

Notes

Chapter 1: ONE NATION UNDER ALLAH

1. Pipes, Daniel. *Conquering America.*

Chapter 2: ON THE ROAD TO THE NEW WORLD

1. Pfander, C. G. *Balance of the truth*, Villach, Light of life, 1986.
2. Abdel Karim, Khalil.*Al jouzour al Tarikhia Lil Sharia*, Cairo, Sina Publishing, 1990.
3. Pfander, C. G. *Balance of the truth*, Villach, Light of life, 1986.
4. Ibid.
5. Ibid.
6. Ibid.
7. Tajer, Jack. *Acbat Wa Muslimoon.* N.j., ACA, 1984.
8. Ye'or, Bat. *The decline of Eastern Christianity under Islam.* Cranbury Associated Press, 1996.
9. Ibid.
10. Abil-Nasr, Abil Kasim. *Al Nasikh Wal Mansoukh.* Cairo, Al Motanabi.

Chapter 3: ISLAM'S WEAPONS FOR THE ISLAMIZATION OF AMERICA

LYING

1. Tabarah, Afif. *The Spirit of Islam.* Beirut, Dar El-Ilm Lilmalayn, 1988.
2. Ibn Hisham. *Al Sira Al Nabawia.* Beirut, Dar Al Wifak, 1955.
3. Ibid.
4. Al Ghazali, Mohammed. *Ehia Ouloum Al-Din.* Dar Al Jil.
5. Ibid.
6. Ibid.
7. Ibid.

SEX

1. Al Askalani. *Kitab Al Nikah,* Beirut
2. Cati, W.I. *Married to Mohammed.* Lake Mary, Creation House Press, 2001.
3. Ibid.

RACE

1. Adams, Moody. *The religion that is raping America.* The Moody Adams Evangelistic Association, 1996.
2. Ibid.
3. Ibid

MONEY

1. Madany, Bassam. *Islam is more than a religion.*
2. Ye'or, Bat. *The decline of Eastern Christianity under Islam.* Cranbury Associated Press, 1996.
3. The Barnabas Fund. *Global Islamic Funding: A challenge to the Church.*
4. Ibid.
5. Ibid.
6. Ibid.
7. Ibid.
8. Ibid.
9. Ibid.
10. Mordecai, Victor. *Is Fanatic Islam a Global threat?* Taylors, 1997.
11. Reed, Stanly. *Following the terrorists' money.*
12. Rotella, Sebastian. *Saudis Must Stem Cash for Terror, Report Says.*
13. Hanson, *Victor Davis. Saudi Arabia Finances Palestinian Genocide.*
14. Marquis, *Christopher. Worried Saudis pay Millions to improve Image in U.S.*
15. Ibid.
16. Ibid.

TERROR

1. McKenzie, Glenn. Nigeria calls for death of writer.
2. Dareini, Ali Akbar. *Scholar sentenced to death in Iran.*
3. www.nawalsaadawi.net/articles/amnesty27-7.htm
4. Ibid.
5. Anderson, John Ward. *In Bangladesh, militants seek writer's death.*
6. Puente, Sonia. Naguib Mahfouz's "*Sanna helwa.*"
7. Al-Akhbar Archives. *Remembering Egypt's Cassandra.*
8. www.kirjasto.sci.fi/rushdie.htm
9. Ibn Hisham. *Al Sira Al Nabawia.* Beirut, Dar Al Wifak, 1955.
10. Ibid.
11. Ibid.

Conclusion

1. Croft, Jim. *Islamic Terrorism*

Bibliography

Arabic Books

- Abil-Nasr, Abil-Kasim. *Al-Nasikh Wal- Mansoukh.* Cairo, Al-Motanabi.
- Al-Ghazali, Mohammed. *Ehia Ouloum -Addin.* Beirut, Dar el-Jil.
- Al-Askalani. *Kitab al-Nikah.* Beirut, Dar al-Balagha, 1986.
- Al-Makdisi. *Fikh al-Irhab.*
- Al-Seuoti. *Asbab al-Nizool.* Beirut, Dar al-Kotib al-Elmia,
- Ibn Hisham. *Al-Sira Al-Nabawia.* Beirut, Dar el-Wifak, 1955.
- Ibn Kathir. *Tafsir al-Quran al-Azim.* Beirut, Dar al-Khair, 1996.

English Books

- Adams, Moody. The religion that is raping America. The Moody Adams Evangelistic Association, 1996.
- Cati, W. L. Married to Mohammed. Lake Mary, Florida, Creation House Press, 2001.
- Croft, Jim. The Muslim Masquerade. Boca Raton, Florida, Jim Croft Ministries, 2002.
- Dashti, Ali. 23 Years. London, George Allen & Unwin, 1985.
- Fregosi, Paul. Jihad. New York, Prometheus Books, 1998.
- Gabriel, Mark. Islam and Terrorism. Lake Mary, Florida, 2002.
- Mikhail, Labib. Islam, Mohammed and the Koran. Blessed Hope Ministries, Spring Field, Virginia, 2002.
- Mordecai, Victor. Is Fanatic Islam a Global Threat? Taylors, 1997.
- Morey, Robert. Winning the War Against Radical Islam. Las Vegas, Christian Scholars Press, 2002.
- Morey, Robert. The Islamic Invasion. Las Vegas, Christian Scholars Press, 1992.
- Pfander, C. G. Balance of Truth. Villach, Light of Life, 1986.
- Shorrosh, Anis. Islam Revealed. Nashville, Thomas Nelson, 1988.
- Ye'or, Bat. The Decline of Eastern Christianity under Islam. Cranbury, Associated Press, 1996.